William J. O'Neil

How to
Make
Money
in
Stocks
DESK DIARY
2 0 0 4

WILEY

John Wiley & Sons, Inc.

For general information on our other products and services, or technical support, please contact our Customer Care Department within the United States at 800-762-2974, outside the United States at 317-572-3993 or fax 317-572-4002.

Wiley also publishes its books in a variety of electronic formats. Some content that appears in print may not be available in electronic books.

For more information about Wiley products, visit our web site at www.wiley.com.

ISBN: 0-471-65092-7

Printed in the United States of America

10 9 8 7 6 5 4 3 2 1

Foreword

My experience teaching thousands of individual investors about the stock market has given me the opportunity to observe first-hand how human beings perceive, absorb, and ultimately learn new information and skills. The stock market, in particular, is a complex beast, and developing proficiency in sound investment methods is a challenging task that requires determination, patience, persistence, and good old elbow grease. In other words, it's hard work! To be successful in the stock market, an investor must be willing to make the effort required to study, learn and refine key investment skills.

When we first created *Investor's Business Daily*, we began to realize that the use of such a sophisticated investment tool by individual investors would require ongoing educational programs. Over the years, we have developed our very successful Advanced Investment Workshops and a variety of tapes and books designed to help our readers understand and utilize effectively the powerful tool that IBD™ and CAN SLIM™ represent in tandem.

Psychological studies have shown that human beings need to be exposed to something three times before it even registers in their brain, and seven times before they learn it cold. This is no different for CAN SLIM and IBD. We have observed that individuals use our methods proficiently only after a period of study and practice, and, in fact, many of the most successful individual investors I have met tell me that they read my book, *How to Make Money in Stocks* several times before the methods outlined in the book really began to make sense and became second nature to them.

With this in mind, we set out to create the investment desk diary you now hold in your hands. Each daily diary entry encapsulates a single small concept, idea, or example relevant to the CAN SLIM investment methodology. By constant, daily reinforcement of these concepts, ideas, and examples, the reader will hopefully be able to better absorb and retain this information. If you have read any of our three books, listened to our tapes, read the Investor's Corner column in IBD, or attended any of our seminars or paid workshops, then it is our hope that this daily diary will help reinforce and solidify the concepts and skills you have learned, and ultimately make you a more successful investor.

My heartfelt thanks goes out to the team who put in many hours of hard work in order to complete this project. In particular, I am grateful to Gil Morales, Gary Flam, Angela Han and Sarah Schneider for their very important contributions.

William J. O'Neil

MONDAY
29
DECEMBER
2003

"If you own two or three stocks that vary in their strength from day to day, resist the temptation to try to trade them back and forth in order to take advantage of this minor performance difference. If you have two or three strongly acting stocks that vary in strength over cycles of a few days, just sit!"

Stocks to Watch			Today's Trades			
Name	Symbol	Pivot Price	Name	Symbol	Quantity	Price

TUESDAY
30
DECEMBER
2003

"As the market is coming down, sometimes a subtle clue that a bottom is forming will show up in that the Accumulation/Distribution Rating of one of the major indexes will be improving as the index is coming down - this occurred in March, 2003 and marked the beginning of a turn to the upside at that point."

Stocks to Watch			Today's Trades			
Name	Symbol	Pivot Price	Name	Symbol	Quantity	Price

WEDNESDAY
31
DECEMBER
2003

"In the market, everything sells for about what its worth at the time. Opinions about how 'fairly valued' a stock or the general market is are just that - opinions. Generally, it is these opinons themselves that are truly 'overvalued.'"

Stocks to Watch			Today's Trades			
Name	Symbol	Pivot Price	Name	Symbol	Quantity	Price
_____	_____	_____	_____	_____	_____	_____
_____	_____	_____	_____	_____	_____	_____
_____	_____	_____	_____	_____	_____	_____

THURSDAY
1
JANUARY
2004

"January is always a strange, volatile month for the market. You're better off taking a vacation."

**U.S. equity markets closed
in observance of New Year's Day.**

"The first step in learning to pick big stock market winners is to examine leading big winners of the past."

Stocks to Watch			Today's Trades			
Name	Symbol	Pivot Price	Name	Symbol	Quantity	Price

"Think of a 7-8% loss-cutting rule as a form of insurance that protects you from disaster. Remember, a 33% loss in your portfolio requires a 50% gain to get even, while a 50% loss requires a 100% gain to get even. When you are wrong, cut your loss quickly to avoid disaster!"

Stocks to Watch			Stocks to Watch		
Name	Symbol	Pivot Price	Name	Symbol	Pivot Price

"You'll never sell at the exact top, so don't kick yourself if a stock goes still higher after you sell. The secret is to hop off the elevator on one of the top floors on the way up and not ride it back down."

Stocks to Watch			Today's Trades			
Name	Symbol	Pivot Price	Name	Symbol	Quantity	Price

"On this day in 1967, Control Data Corporation, a developer of high-speed digital computers, busted out of a 14-week cup-with-handle base, and in 42 weeks vaulted 358% from its pivot point."

Control Data Corporation Weekly Chart   **1967**

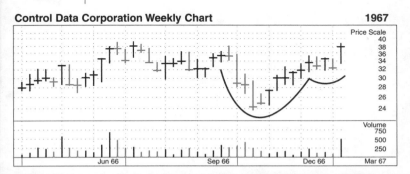

Stocks to Watch			Today's Trades			
Name	Symbol	Pivot Price	Name	Symbol	Quantity	Price

"Always sell your losers and mistakes, and watch your better selections to see if they progress into your big winners."

Stocks to Watch			Today's Trades			
Name	Symbol	Pivot Price	Name	Symbol	Quantity	Price

"On this day in 1999, Qualcomm, Inc. blasted out of a 23-week cup-with-handle base and shot up 2,556% over the next 57 weeks."

Qualcomm Inc Weekly Chart   **1999**

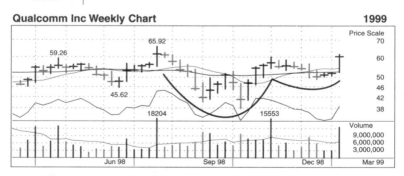

Stocks to Watch			Today's Trades			
Name	Symbol	Pivot Price	Name	Symbol	Quantity	Price

FRIDAY
9
JANUARY
2004

"The best results are usually achieved through concentration, by putting your eggs in a few baskets you know well and watch very carefully."

Stocks to Watch			Today's Trades			
Name	Symbol	Pivot Price	Name	Symbol	Quantity	Price

SAT/SUN
10/11
JANUARY
2004

"In bear markets, stocks usually open strong and close weak. In bull markets, they tend to open weak and close strong."

Stocks to Watch			Stocks to Watch		
Name	Symbol	Pivot Price	Name	Symbol	Pivot Price

MONDAY
12
JANUARY
2004

"If you miss a stock's initial breakout from a cup-with-handle, you should keep your eye on it. In time, it may form a flat base and give you another opportunity to buy."

Limited Brands Inc Weekly Chart   **1985**

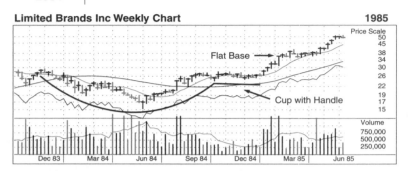

Stocks to Watch			Today's Trades			
Name	Symbol	Pivot Price	Name	Symbol	Quantity	Price

TUESDAY
13
JANUARY
2004

"A stock that moves higher while volume trends lower suggests that big investors have lost their appetite for the stock and therefore the stock may be topping."

Stocks to Watch			Today's Trades			
Name	Symbol	Pivot Price	Name	Symbol	Quantity	Price

WEDNESDAY

14

**JANUARY
2004**

"On this day in 1965, Polaroid Corporation, riding the inno- vative success of its revolutionary instant photo-developing camera, emerged from a 16-month cup-with-handle base and began a 35-month, 440% run."

Polaroid Corporation Weekly Chart   **1965**

| Price Scale |
| 190 |
| 170 |
| 150 |
| 130 |

172.50

145.25

129.50

133.13

Volume
120,000
80,000
40,000

75,000   68,000

Mar 64   Jun 64   Sep 64   Dec 64   Mar 65

Stocks to Watch				**Today's Trades**			
Name	Symbol	Pivot Price		Name	Symbol	Quantity	Price

THURSDAY

15

**JANUARY
2004**

"A price drop in a proper handle should be contained within 10% to 15% of its peak unless the stock forms a very large cup. However if you are in a period of unusual general market weakness then some handle areas can quickly decline around 20% to 30%, but the price pattern can still be sound."

America Online Inc Weekly Chart   **1998**

Deep handle due to extreme
market volatility in October 1998

| Price Scale |
| 130 |
| 110 |
| 100 |
| 90 |
| 80 |
| 70 |
| 60 |
| 46 |

Cup with handle base

Volume
30,000,000
20,000,000
10,000,000

Mar 98   Jun 98   Sep 98   Dec 98

Stocks to Watch				**Today's Trades**			
Name	Symbol	Pivot Price		Name	Symbol	Quantity	Price

"If your stock's RS rating is below 70, it is lagging the better-performing stocks in the overall market. That doesn't mean it can't go up in price—it just means that if by some chance it does go up, it'll probably go up less."

Stocks to Watch			Today's Trades			
Name	Symbol	Pivot Price	Name	Symbol	Quantity	Price

"Strong, improved quarterly earnings should always be supported by sales growth of at least 25% for the latest quarter, or at least an acceleration in the rate of sales percentage improvement per the last three quarters."

Stocks to Watch			Stocks to Watch		
Name	Symbol	Pivot Price	Name	Symbol	Pivot Price

MONDAY
19
**JANUARY
2004**

"Most (investors) average down, meaning they buy additional shares as a stock declines in price in order to lower their cost per share. But why add more of your hard-earned money to stocks that aren't working?"

Enron Corp Weekly Chart   **1985**

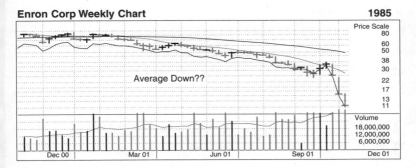

U.S. equity markets closed in observance of Martin Luther King, Jr. Day.

TUESDAY
20
**JANUARY
2004**

"The general market averages need to be studied closely every day since reverses in trends can begin on any given day."

Stocks to Watch			Today's Trades			
Name	Symbol	Pivot Price	Name	Symbol	Quantity	Price

WEDNESDAY

21

JANUARY
2004

"An indication of a top can be seen on a daily chart when a stock will, for several days, close at or near the lows of the daily price ranges, fully retracing the day's advances with volume picking up."

Nucor Corp Daily Chart   **2002**

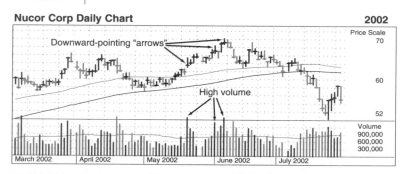

Stocks to Watch			Today's Trades			
Name	Symbol	Pivot Price	Name	Symbol	Quantity	Price

THURSDAY

22

JANUARY
2004

"It also helps improve your batting average if your stock selections show the latest quarter's after-tax profit margins are either at, or near a new high."

Stocks to Watch			Today's Trades			
Name	Symbol	Pivot Price	Name	Symbol	Quantity	Price

"On this day in 1967, nine-week old IPO Digital Equipment Corp., a manufacturer of small, high-speed digital computers, popped out of a six-week flat base to begin a run that took it 351% higher over the next 46 weeks."

Digital Equipment Corp Weekly Chart   **1967**

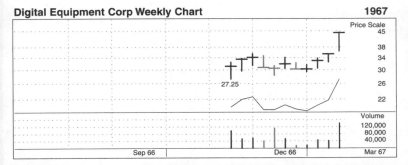

	Stocks to Watch			Today's Trades		
Name	Symbol	Pivot Price	Name	Symbol	Quantity	Price

"Look for abnormal strength in a weak market."

	Stocks to Watch			Stocks to Watch	
Name	Symbol	Pivot Price	Name	Symbol	Pivot Price

MONDAY
26
JANUARY
2004

"Two quarters of major earnings deceleration can mean trouble. By this I mean if a company is growing quarterly earnings at a 50% rate and suddenly reports earnings gains of only 15%, that usually spells trouble and you probably want to avoid it."

Stocks to Watch				Today's Trades			
Name	Symbol	Pivot Price		Name	Symbol	Quantity	Price

TUESDAY
27
JANUARY
2004

"A 'flat base' is usually a second-stage base that occurs after the stock has advanced 20% or more off a cup-with-handle, saucer, or double bottom. This base moves straight sideways in a fairly tight price range for at least five or six weeks, and it does not correct more than 10% to 15%."

Cisco Systems Inc Weekly Chart   **1999**

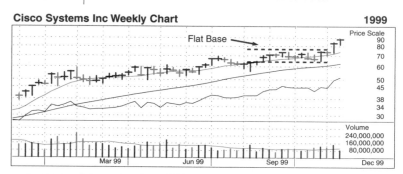

Stocks to Watch				Today's Trades			
Name	Symbol	Pivot Price		Name	Symbol	Quantity	Price

WEDNESDAY

28

JANUARY
2004

"The winning investor's objective should be to have one or two big winners rather than dozens of very small profits."

Stocks to Watch			Today's Trades			
Name	Symbol	Pivot Price	Name	Symbol	Quantity	Price

THURSDAY

29

JANUARY
2004

"Do not get caught up in what others say or do. Stick to your own analysis and parameters and operate off of those—don't get distracted by others' opinions!"

Stocks to Watch			Today's Trades			
Name	Symbol	Pivot Price	Name	Symbol	Quantity	Price

NOTES:

NOTES:

FRIDAY
30
JANUARY
2004

"On this day in 1995, five-month old IPO Accustaff emerged from an 18-week cup-with-handle formation and began a 68-week romp that sent the stock up over 1,486%."

Accustaff Inc Weekly Chart   **1995**

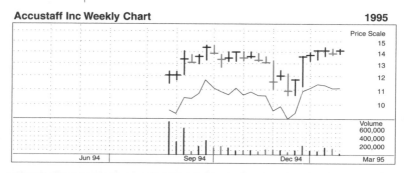

Stocks to Watch			Today's Trades			
Name	Symbol	Pivot Price	Name	Symbol	Quantity	Price

SAT/SUN
31/1
JAN/FEB
2004

"In most cases, if you own a big, powerful leader, you should hold it until it actually does have a climax run—that is your sell signal."

Schwab Charles Corp Daily Chart   **1999**

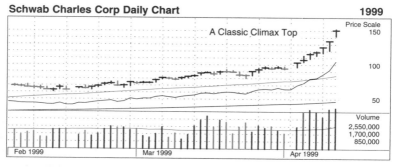

A Classic Climax Top

Stocks to Watch			Stocks to Watch		
Name	Symbol	Pivot Price	Name	Symbol	Pivot Price

"Our ongoing analysis of the most successful stocks from 1952 to present shows that P/E ratios were not a relevant factor in price movement and have very little to do with whether a stock should be bought or sold. P/E's are an end effect, not a cause."

Stocks to Watch			Today's Trades			
Name	Symbol	Pivot Price	Name	Symbol	Quantity	Price

"Wide and loose looking charts usually fail but can tighten up later."

Ebay Inc Weekly Chart   **2003**

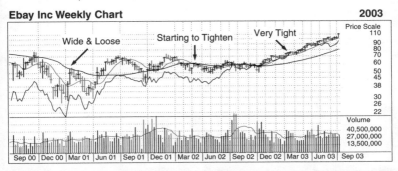

Stocks to Watch			Today's Trades			
Name	Symbol	Pivot Price	Name	Symbol	Quantity	Price

"Pros Make Mistakes Too—Many professional investment managers make the serious mistake of buying stocks that have just suffered unusually large price drops. As our studies indicate, this is a surefire way to get yourself in trouble."

Stocks to Watch			Today's Trades			
Name	Symbol	Pivot Price	Name	Symbol	Quantity	Price

"Sometimes, after a climax run, a stock will fall sharply, then turn and rally rapidly as much as 10% beyond its previous price peak—this is your last chance to sell."

Emulex Corp Weekly Chart   **2000**

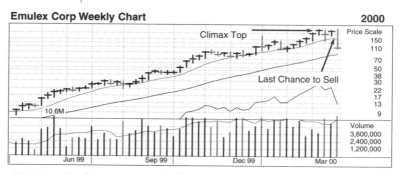

Stocks to Watch			Today's Trades			
Name	Symbol	Pivot Price	Name	Symbol	Quantity	Price

"Much like doctors do postmortem operations and the Civil Aeronautics Board conducts postcrash investigations, investors should mark every buy and sell point on a chart and analyze the decisions they have made so they can learn from them."

Stocks to Watch			Today's Trades			
Name	Symbol	Pivot Price	Name	Symbol	Quantity	Price

"On February 7, 1958 bowling ball maker Brunswick Corp. emerged from a 25-week cup-with-handle base and ran 1,233% in 38-months."

Brunswick Corp Weekly Chart   **1958**

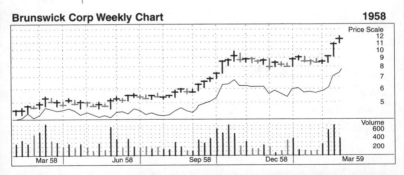

Stocks to Watch			Stocks to Watch		
Name	Symbol	Pivot Price	Name	Symbol	Pivot Price

MONDAY
9
FEBRUARY
2004

"The pivot buy point in a double bottom is located on the top right side of the 'W' where the stock is coming up after the second leg down. The pivot point should be equal in price to the top of the middle peak of the 'W'."

American Power Conversion Corp Weekly Chart   **1990**

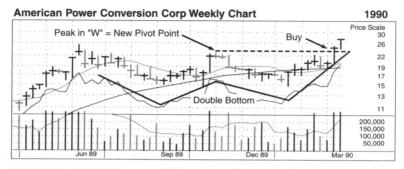

Stocks to Watch			Today's Trades			
Name	Symbol	Pivot Price	Name	Symbol	Quantity	Price

TUESDAY
10
FEBRUARY
2004

"Before their major run-ups, the best-performing stocks each year from the early 1950's through 2000 had an average RS Rating of 87. So the determined winner's rule: Avoid laggard stocks and sympathy moves. Look for the genuine leaders."

Stocks to Watch			Today's Trades			
Name	Symbol	Pivot Price	Name	Symbol	Quantity	Price

"Poor relative strength can be a reason for selling. Consider selling when a stock's IBD's Relative Price Strength Rating drops below 70."

Stocks to Watch			Today's Trades			
Name	Symbol	Pivot Price	Name	Symbol	Quantity	Price

"Our analysis of the most successful stocks showed that, in almost every case, earnings growth accelerated some time in the 10 quarters before a towering price move began. If a company's earnings are up 15% a year and suddenly begin spurting 40% to 50 % or more, it usually creates the conditions for important stock price movement."

Stocks to Watch			Today's Trades			
Name	Symbol	Pivot Price	Name	Symbol	Quantity	Price

"A stock chart base with only two weeks down in the left side is characteristic of an improper base. Four to five weeks on the left side allows the psychology to set up correctly by shaking out ALL the weak holders before the stock moves up."

Stocks to Watch			Today's Trades			
Name	Symbol	Pivot Price	Name	Symbol	Quantity	Price

"When averaging up on a position, once you get away from the initial base breakout, keep your average cost 20-30% below where the stock is currently trading."

Stocks to Watch			Stocks to Watch		
Name	Symbol	Pivot Price	Name	Symbol	Pivot Price

"The 'two down and two up' sell signal: if a stock has an extended run of approximately five months or more (not just a few
weeks), moves into new high ground, then pulls back sharply for
one to three weeks and then goes straight back into new high
ground, 75% of the time it can just be sold right there."

EMC Corp Weekly Chart   **1993**

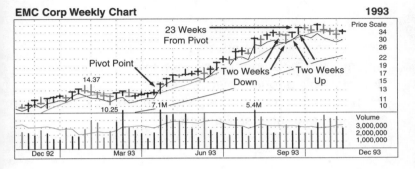

U.S. equity markets closed
in observance of Presidents' Day.

"On February 17, 1965, KLM Royal Dutch Airlines, on the
wings of a new era of jet travel, took off from a 45-week cup-
with-handle base after one failed break-out attempt that was
contained to within 8% of its pivot point, and over the next
14 months flew 4,719% higher."

KLM Royal Dutch Airlines Weekly Chart   **1965**

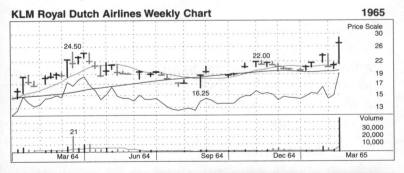

Stocks to Watch			Today's Trades			
Name	Symbol	Pivot Price	Name	Symbol	Quantity	Price
___	___	___	___	___	___	___
___	___	___	___	___	___	___
___	___	___	___	___	___	___

"Investment newsletters can create doubt, uncertainty, and confusion in an investor's mind. Interestingly enough, history shows that the market tends to go up just when these experts are most skeptical and uncertain."

Stocks to Watch			Today's Trades			
Name	Symbol	Pivot Price	Name	Symbol	Quantity	Price

"A thin stock can act wild and close in the middle or lower part of its range on a daily basis and still be okay. The wild action is not necessarily a sign of weakness as much as it is a sign of the stock's 'thinness.'"

Stocks to Watch			Today's Trades			
Name	Symbol	Pivot Price	Name	Symbol	Quantity	Price

"From 1953 to 1985, the average P/E ratio for the best-performing stocks at their early emerging stage was 20. While advancing, the biggest winners expanded their P/E's by 125% to about 45."

Stocks to Watch			Today's Trades			
Name	Symbol	Pivot Price	Name	Symbol	Quantity	Price

"In a study done in 1995, we found that if a big leader from one bull cycle corrected more than 89% in the ensuing bear period then it NEVER came back in price—proving that the cheaper they look, the more expensive they can be!"

Stocks to Watch			Stocks to Watch		
Name	Symbol	Pivot Price	Name	Symbol	Pivot Price

MONDAY

23

FEBRUARY
2004

"It doesn't pay to argue with the market. Experience teaches that fighting the market can be a very expensive lesson."

Stocks to Watch			Today's Trades			
Name	Symbol	Pivot Price	Name	Symbol	Quantity	Price

TUESDAY

24

FEBRUARY
2004

"Before turning negative on a company's earnings, I prefer two quarters of material slowdown, usually a two-third decline from the prior several quarters' rate of growth. One quarter down is okay as even the best organizations can have one slow quarter every once in a while."

Stocks to Watch			Today's Trades			
Name	Symbol	Pivot Price	Name	Symbol	Quantity	Price

"Look on a chart for the relative strength line. If it has been sinking for seven months or more, or if the line has an abnormally sharp decline for four months or more, the stock's price behavior is highly questionable."

Stocks to Watch			Today's Trades			
Name	Symbol	Pivot Price	Name	Symbol	Quantity	Price

"Our studies show that the most reliable base patterns must have a minimum of seven to eight weeks of price consolidation."

Stocks to Watch			Today's Trades			
Name	Symbol	Pivot Price	Name	Symbol	Quantity	Price

FRIDAY

27

**FEBRUARY
2004**

"In a double bottom pattern (looks like the letter 'W') it is usually important that the second bottom of the 'W' match the price level (low) of the first bottom or, as in most cases, undercut it by one or two points, thereby creating a shakeout of weaker investors."

Nokia Corp Ads Weekly Chart   **1998**

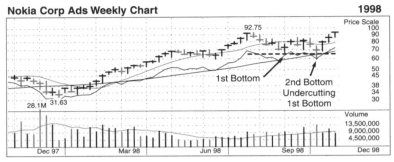

Stocks to Watch			Today's Trades			
Name	Symbol	Pivot Price	Name	Symbol	Quantity	Price

SAT/SUN

28/29

**FEBRUARY
2004**

"On February 28, 1957, Zenith Radio Corp., riding the new wave of color television, broke out of an 11-week cup-with-handle base and powered 511% higher over the next 66 weeks."

Zenith Radio Corp Weekly Chart   **1957**

Stocks to Watch			Stocks to Watch		
Name	Symbol	Pivot Price	Name	Symbol	Pivot Price

"I do not like to buy any stock that sells below $15 per share, and neither should you. Our studies of super winners show that most broke out of chart bases between $30 and $50 a share."

Stocks to Watch			Today's Trades			
Name	Symbol	Pivot Price	Name	Symbol	Quantity	Price

"An individual investor can afford to wait for a company to show real earnings improvement. Requiring that current quarterly earnings be up a hefty amount is just another smart way the intelligent investor can reduce the risk of mistakes in stock selection."

Stocks to Watch			Today's Trades			
Name	Symbol	Pivot Price	Name	Symbol	Quantity	Price

NOTES:

"Restrict your purchases to companies showing a Relative Price Strength Rating of 80 or higher. There's no point to buying a stock that's straggling behind many others in the market."

Stocks to Watch			Today's Trades			
Name	Symbol	Pivot Price	Name	Symbol	Quantity	Price

"Plot out your mistakes on charts, study them, and write some additional rules in order to correct your mistakes and the actions that cost you money."

Stocks to Watch			Today's Trades			
Name	Symbol	Pivot Price	Name	Symbol	Quantity	Price

"If a stock already has made an extended advance and suddenly makes its greatest one-day price drop since the beginning of the move, consider selling if confirmed by other signals."

Stocks to Watch			Today's Trades			
Name	Symbol	Pivot Price	Name	Symbol	Quantity	Price

"The importance of knowing the direction of the general market cannot be overemphasized. A 33% loss in a portfolio of stocks requires a 50% gain just to get to your break-even point."

Stocks to Watch			Stocks to Watch		
Name	Symbol	Pivot Price	Name	Symbol	Pivot Price

MONDAY

8

**MARCH
2004**

"Double bottoms may also have handles—with a depth and length similar to those found in a cup-with-handle—although this is not essential. If the double bottom has a handle, then the peak price of the handle is the pivot buy point."

N V R Inc Weekly Chart   **2001**

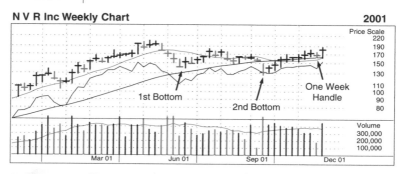

Stocks to Watch			Today's Trades			
Name	Symbol	Pivot Price	Name	Symbol	Quantity	Price

TUESDAY

9

**MARCH
2004**

"Logarithmic-scale graphs are of great value in analyzing stocks because acceleration or deceleration in the percentage rate of quarterly earnings increases can be seen very clearly, since one inch anywhere on the price of the earnings scale represents the same percentage change."

Stocks to Watch			Today's Trades			
Name	Symbol	Pivot Price	Name	Symbol	Quantity	Price

WEDNESDAY
10
MARCH
2004

"Head and shoulders top patterns are one of the more reliable patterns—the right shoulder must be slightly below the left shoulder."

Lucent Technologies Inc Weekly Chart   **2000**

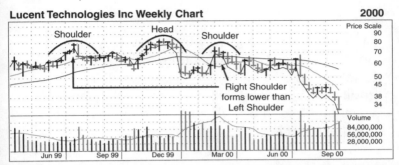

Stocks to Watch			Today's Trades			
Name	Symbol	Pivot Price	Name	Symbol	Quantity	Price

THURSDAY
11
MARCH
2004

"On this day in 1968, Skyline Corp., riding the new wave of mobile homes and travel trailers, came out of a short, eight-week cup-with-handle and traveled 1,160% higher over the next 41 weeks."

Skyline Corp Weekly Chart   **1968**

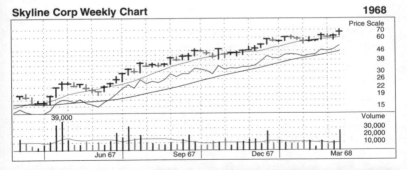

Stocks to Watch			Today's Trades			
Name	Symbol	Pivot Price	Name	Symbol	Quantity	Price

"In a bull market, one way to maneuver your portfolio toward more concentrated positions is to follow up and make one or two smaller additional buys in stocks as soon as they have advanced 2% to 3% above your original or last purchase price."

Stocks to Watch			Today's Trades			
Name	Symbol	Pivot Price	Name	Symbol	Quantity	Price

"Look ahead to the next quarter or two and check the earnings that were reported for those same quarters the previous year. If unusually large or small results in the year-earlier period are not due to extraordinary items, it may help you anticipate a strong or poor earnings report in the coming months."

Stocks to Watch			Stocks to Watch		
Name	Symbol	Pivot Price	Name	Symbol	Pivot Price

MONDAY

15

MARCH
2004

"A head and shoulders bottom may succeed in a
few cases, but it has no strong prior uptrend, which
is essential for most powerful market leaders."

Stocks to Watch			Today's Trades			
Name	Symbol	Pivot Price	Name	Symbol	Quantity	Price

TUESDAY

16

MARCH
2004

"On this day in 1999, Adobe Systems, creator of the Adobe
Acrobat document reader that enabled transmission of
print-quality documents over the Internet, began an 86-week
move that took the stock 596% higher."

Adobe Systems Inc Weekly Chart   **1999**

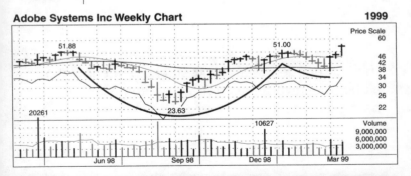

Stocks to Watch			Today's Trades			
Name	Symbol	Pivot Price	Name	Symbol	Quantity	Price

WEDNESDAY
17
MARCH
2004

"Consider selling if a stock breaks down on the largest weekly volume in its prior several years."

Tyco International Ltd Weekly Chart   **1999**

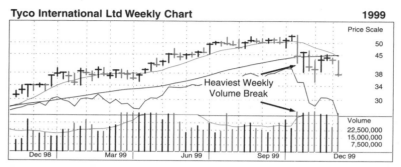

Price Scale
50
45
38
34
30

Heaviest Weekly Volume Break

Volume
22,500,000
15,000,000
7,500,000

Dec 98   Mar 99   Jun 99   Sep 99   Dec 99

Stocks to Watch			Today's Trades			
Name	Symbol	Pivot Price	Name	Symbol	Quantity	Price

THURSDAY
18
MARCH
2004

"It's not enough to just buy stocks that show the highest relative price strength on some list of best performers."

Stocks to Watch			Today's Trades			
Name	Symbol	Pivot Price	Name	Symbol	Quantity	Price

"On this day in 1982, Nasdaq new issue Home Depot emerged from an eight-week base and began a 10-fold, 12-month price run."

Home Depot Inc Weekly Chart   **1982**

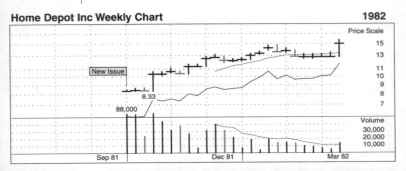

Stocks to Watch			Today's Trades			
Name	Symbol	Pivot Price	Name	Symbol	Quantity	Price

"If a stock is so powerful that it vaults 20% in just one, two, or three weeks from a sound breakout, the stock has to be held at least eight weeks."

Stocks to Watch			Stocks to Watch		
Name	Symbol	Pivot Price	Name	Symbol	Pivot Price

"Overconcern about taxes can confuse and cloud normally sound investment judgement. The investment decision should always be considered first and tax considerations made a distant second."

Stocks to Watch			Today's Trades			
Name	Symbol	Pivot Price	Name	Symbol	Quantity	Price

"On this day in 1994, Microsoft signaled the start of the personal computer's status as the vehicle of choice for the Internet age by breaking out of a 27-week flat base and marching 569% higher over the next 169 weeks."

Microsoft Corp Weekly Chart   **1994**

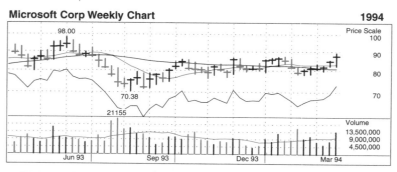

Stocks to Watch			Today's Trades			
Name	Symbol	Pivot Price	Name	Symbol	Quantity	Price

"Overhead supply occurs when a stock moves up to a price area where a lot of trades occurred on the way down, creating willing sellers who bought the stock at these levels, watched it tank, and now want to 'get out even.'"

Qlogic Corp Weekly Chart   **2001**

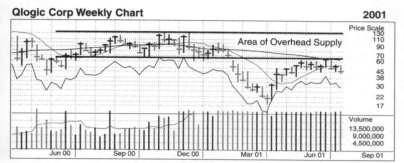

Stocks to Watch				Today's Trades			
Name	Symbol	Pivot Price		Name	Symbol	Quantity	Price

"Buy companies that show increasing sponsorship. The main thing to look for is the recent quarterly trend. It's always best to buy stocks showing an increasing number of institutional owners over several recent quarters."

Stocks to Watch				Today's Trades			
Name	Symbol	Pivot Price		Name	Symbol	Quantity	Price

"When you average up on a position by buying some stock on the way up, if the stock starts to come off and it perhaps isn't looking too good, then sell the portion that you just bought. In other words, don't let that new part of the position get too far underwater."

Stocks to Watch		
Name	Symbol	Pivot Price

Today's Trades			
Name	Symbol	Quantity	Price

"Check the earnings of other companies in your stock's industry group. If you can't find one or two other impressive stocks in the group displaying strong earnings, chances are you may have selected the wrong investment."

Stocks to Watch		
Name	Symbol	Pivot Price

Stocks to Watch		
Name	Symbol	Pivot Price

"After a prolonged upswing, if a stock's 200-day moving average price line turns down, consider selling the stock."

Stocks to Watch			Today's Trades			
Name	Symbol	Pivot Price	Name	Symbol	Quantity	Price

"The really big money-making stock selections generally have RS Ratings of 90 or higher just before breaking out of their first or second base structure."

Stocks to Watch			Today's Trades			
Name	Symbol	Pivot Price	Name	Symbol	Quantity	Price

NOTES:

NOTES:

WEDNESDAY
31
MARCH
2004

"A saucer with handle is a price pattern similar to the cup-with-handle except that the 'saucer' part tends to stretch out over a longer period of time, making the pattern more shallow."

Delta Airlines Inc Weekly Chart   **1965**

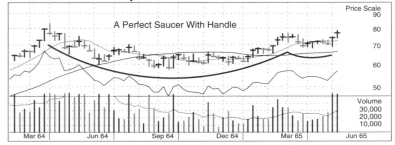

Stocks to Watch			Today's Trades			
Name	Symbol	Pivot Price	Name	Symbol	Quantity	Price

THURSDAY
1
APRIL
2004

"If you are not willing to pay an average of 25 to 50 times earnings or even much more for growth stocks, you have automatically eliminated most of the best investments available (i.e. MSFT, CSCO, HD, and AOL)."

Stocks to Watch			Today's Trades			
Name	Symbol	Pivot Price	Name	Symbol	Quantity	Price

"Set a minimum level for current earnings increases of 25% to 30%. To be even safer, insist that both of the last two quarters show powerful earnings gains—from 40% to 500% or more."

Stocks to Watch			Today's Trades			
Name	Symbol	Pivot Price	Name	Symbol	Quantity	Price

"On this day in 1963, shares of Xerox Corporation, creator of a new document duplication technology that would later transform the company's name into a widely-used verb, popped out of a 12-week cup-with-handle base to begin a 39-month run that took the stock up 718%."

Xerox Corp Weekly Chart

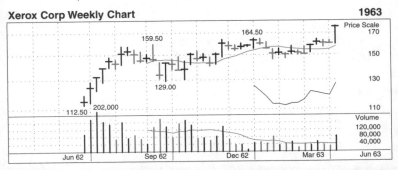

Stocks to Watch			Stocks to Watch		
Name	Symbol	Pivot Price	Name	Symbol	Pivot Price

"Avoid sympathy stock moves, where a lower-ranked stock in the same group as the leading company is bought in hope that the leader's luster will rub off onto it. Eventually they'll try to move up 'in sympathy' with the real leader, but they never do as well."

Stocks to Watch			Today's Trades			
Name	Symbol	Pivot Price	Name	Symbol	Quantity	Price

"Alert investors should keep track of all new stock issues that have emerged over the last one to eight years. This is important because some of the newer and younger companies will be among the most stunning performers of the next year or two."

Stocks to Watch			Today's Trades			
Name	Symbol	Pivot Price	Name	Symbol	Quantity	Price

"The time between your buy and sell could be either short or long. Let your rules and the market decide which one it is."

Stocks to Watch			Today's Trades			
Name	Symbol	Pivot Price	Name	Symbol	Quantity	Price

"When it's exciting and obvious to everyone that a stock is going higher, sell, because it is too late!"

Stocks to Watch			Today's Trades			
Name	Symbol	Pivot Price	Name	Symbol	Quantity	Price

"If you get discouraged, don't ever give up. Go back and put in some detailed extra effort. It's always the study and time you put in after nine to five, Monday through Friday, that ultimately make the difference between winning and losing in the market."

U.S. equity markets closed in observance of Good Friday.

"Never buy a stock solely because the P/E ratio makes it look like a bargain. There are usually good reasons why P/E's are so low, and there is no golden rule in the stock market that protects a stock that sells at 8 or 10 times earnings from going even lower and selling at 4 or 5 times earnings."

Stocks to Watch		
Name	Symbol	Pivot Price

Stocks to Watch		
Name	Symbol	Pivot Price

MONDAY
12
APRIL
2004

"Consider selling if a stock has had a long advance, then closes below its 10-week moving average and lives there for many weeks below that average, unable to rally."

Stocks to Watch			Today's Trades			
Name	Symbol	Pivot Price	Name	Symbol	Quantity	Price

TUESDAY
13
APRIL
2004

"A key concept in climax tops: keep in mind where you are in the total move. What looks like a climax top at the beginning of a stock's move probably isn't."

Qualcomm Inc Weekly Chart   **1999**

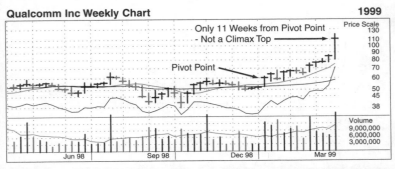

Stocks to Watch			Today's Trades			
Name	Symbol	Pivot Price	Name	Symbol	Quantity	Price

"During the 1990-95 period, the real leaders began with average P/E of 36 that expanded into the 80s. Since these are averages, the beginning P/E range for most big winners was 25 to 50 and the P/E expansions varied from 60 to 115."

Stocks to Watch			Today's Trades			
Name	Symbol	Pivot Price	Name	Symbol	Quantity	Price

"Relative strength should be up four months off the bottom before you can be very sure that a stock is in turn coming up off of its bottom okay after having been in a downtrend for a long period of time."

Stocks to Watch			Today's Trades			
Name	Symbol	Pivot Price	Name	Symbol	Quantity	Price

"A standout stock needs a sound growth record
during recent years, but also a strong current
earnings record in the last few quarters. It is the
powerful combination of these two critical factors,
rather than one or the other, which creates a
super stock, or at least one that has a higher
chance of true success."

Stocks to Watch			Today's Trades			
Name	Symbol	Pivot Price	Name	Symbol	Quantity	Price

"After you see the first several definite indications
of a market top, don't wait around. Sell quickly
before real weakness develops."

Stocks to Watch			Stocks to Watch		
Name	Symbol	Pivot Price	Name	Symbol	Pivot Price

"The market breathes, or as the great stock speculator Jesse Livermore said, 'Action, reaction, action, reaction.' So let your stocks and the market breathe—don't get shaken out on normal pullbacks."

Stocks to Watch			Today's Trades			
Name	Symbol	Pivot Price	Name	Symbol	Quantity	Price

"Successful, young, high-tech growth stocks tend to enjoy their fastest earnings growth between their fifth and tenth years in business, so keep an eye on them during their early growth periods."

Stocks to Watch			Today's Trades			
Name	Symbol	Pivot Price	Name	Symbol	Quantity	Price

"If an IPO doesn't show a three-year earnings record, look for the last five or six quarterly earnings reports to be up a huge amount and even more quarters of enormous sales increases. One or two quarters of profitability is frequently not enough."

Stocks to Watch			Today's Trades			
Name	Symbol	Pivot Price	Name	Symbol	Quantity	Price

"Our research showed that 80% of the stocks that had outstanding performance in the 1980s and 1990s were ones that had been brought public in the prior few years."

Stocks to Watch			Today's Trades			
Name	Symbol	Pivot Price	Name	Symbol	Quantity	Price

"The winning investor should avoid the trap of being influenced by nonrecurring profits. Omit a company's one-time extraordinary gains such as the sale of real estate."

Stocks to Watch			Today's Trades			
Name	Symbol	Pivot Price	Name	Symbol	Quantity	Price

"Napoleon once wrote that never hesitating in battle gave him an advantage over his opponents, and for many years he was undefeated. In the battlefield that is the stock market there are the quick and there are the dead."

Stocks to Watch			Stocks to Watch		
Name	Symbol	Pivot Price	Name	Symbol	Pivot Price

"If you buy exactly at the right time off a proper daily or weekly chart base in the first place, and you do not chase or pyramid a stock when it's extended in price more than 5% past a correct pivot buy point, you will be in position to sit through most normal corrections."

Stocks to Watch			Today's Trades			
Name	Symbol	Pivot Price	Name	Symbol	Quantity	Price

"Market makers and specialists will accommodate buyers as they raise the price of a stock, possibly even selling out of their own inventory or selling short in order to meet demand. After doing this, the first chance they get they'll knock the stock down to reload inventory or cover their shorts."

Stocks to Watch			Today's Trades			
Name	Symbol	Pivot Price	Name	Symbol	Quantity	Price

WEDNESDAY
28
APRIL
2004

"On this day in 1967, drug store operator Jack Eckerd Corp. amped up and broke out of an over 1-year-long cup-with-handle base to begin a 30-month, 660% move."

Jack Eckerd Corp Weekly Chart   **1967**

	Stocks to Watch			Today's Trades		
Name	Symbol	Pivot Price	Name	Symbol	Quantity	Price

THURSDAY
29
APRIL
2004

"In most cases, sell when quarterly earnings percentage increases slow materially for two consecutive quarters."

	Stocks to Watch			Today's Trades		
Name	Symbol	Pivot Price	Name	Symbol	Quantity	Price

"A bear market is the time to do a post-analysis of prior decisions. Study your decisions and write out some new rules to avoid the mistakes you made in the past cycle."

Stocks to Watch			Today's Trades			
Name	Symbol	Pivot Price	Name	Symbol	Quantity	Price

"The RS Rating of a potential winning stock should be in the same league as a pitcher's fastball. The average big league fastball is clocked about 86 miles per hour, and the best pitchers throw heat in the 90s."

Stocks to Watch			Stocks to Watch		
Name	Symbol	Pivot Price	Name	Symbol	Pivot Price

NOTES:

NOTES:

MONDAY

3

MAY
2004

"Don't trade on news—it can shake you out.
Understand the company and how they are really
doing before reacting to a single news item on
the company."

Stocks to Watch			Today's Trades			
Name	Symbol	Pivot Price	Name	Symbol	Quantity	Price

TUESDAY

4

MAY
2004

"The safest time to buy an IPO is on the breakout
from its first correction and base-building area."

Stocks to Watch			Today's Trades			
Name	Symbol	Pivot Price	Name	Symbol	Quantity	Price

"It seldom pays to invest in laggard stocks, even if they look tantalizingly cheap. Look for, and confine your purchases to, market leaders."

Stocks to Watch			Today's Trades			
Name	Symbol	Pivot Price	Name	Symbol	Quantity	Price

"The great stock speculator Jesse Livermore observed: 'It's not your thinking that makes you money, it's your sitting.' Learn to capture the bulk of a big winner's move by knowing when to sit."

Stocks to Watch			Today's Trades			
Name	Symbol	Pivot Price	Name	Symbol	Quantity	Price

"Rallies in cyclical stocks tend to be short-lived
and tend to falter at the first hint of an earnings
slowdown."

Stocks to Watch		
Name	Symbol	Pivot Price

Today's Trades			
Name	Symbol	Quantity	Price

"The vast majority of superior stocks will rank 80
or higher on both EPS and RS Rating before their
major moves. Since one is a fundamental
measurement and the other is a marketplace
valuation, insisting on both numbers being strong
should, in positive markets, materially improve
your selection process."

Stocks to Watch		
Name	Symbol	Pivot Price

Stocks to Watch		
Name	Symbol	Pivot Price

MONDAY
10
MAY
2004

"When you get out of a bear market you should stay out until the bear market is over."

Stocks to Watch			Today's Trades			
Name	Symbol	Pivot Price	Name	Symbol	Quantity	Price

TUESDAY
11
MAY
2004

"Winning stocks very rarely ever drop 8% below a correct buy pivot point. In fact, most big winners don't close below their pivot point. Buying as close as possible to the pivot point is therefore absolutely essential and may let you cut losses before the stock declines 8% from your buy point."

Stocks to Watch			Today's Trades			
Name	Symbol	Pivot Price	Name	Symbol	Quantity	Price

"When you buy, make absolutely sure the stock is coming out of a sound base (price consolidation area) and that you buy it at its exact pivot buy point. If you can't buy at the exact pivot point, then be sure it's not extended more than 5% above the precise buy point of this base."

Stocks to Watch			Today's Trades			
Name	Symbol	Pivot Price	Name	Symbol	Quantity	Price

"Beating or missing estimates is one thing, but investors should be more interested in the percentage gain or decline in the earnings. Just looking at whether the company missed or beat analysts' earnings estimates is too simplistic."

Stocks to Watch			Today's Trades			
Name	Symbol	Pivot Price	Name	Symbol	Quantity	Price

"When the IBD Mutual Fund Index forms a sound pattern, say a cup-with-handle for instance, this is almost always constructive for the market."

Stocks to Watch			Today's Trades			
Name	Symbol	Pivot Price	Name	Symbol	Quantity	Price

"On May 16, 1995, C-Cube Microsystems, a maker of enabling technology for mpeg videos transmitted over PCs and the Internet, sporting six straight quarters of triple-digit earnings growth, emerged from a 9-month cup-with-handle base formation and rocketed 494% higher over the next 41 weeks."

C Cube Microsystems Inc Weekly Chart   **1995**

Stocks to Watch			Stocks to Watch		
Name	Symbol	Pivot Price	Name	Symbol	Pivot Price

MONDAY

17

MAY
2004

"Don't pay attention to the trade deficit. While economists make a big deal of this, it is more a sign of strength in the U.S. in that we are generating wealth which creates buying power that in turn spills over to buying of foreign goods and services."

Stocks to Watch			Today's Trades			
Name	Symbol	Pivot Price	Name	Symbol	Quantity	Price

TUESDAY

18

MAY
2004

"On this day in 1999, Triquint Semiconductor, expanding the physical limitations of integrated circuits with its proprietary gallium arsenide technology, bounced out of a tight flag pattern and ran up 1,078% over the next 41 weeks."

Triquint Semiconductor Inc Weekly Chart   **1999**

Stocks to Watch			Today's Trades			
Name	Symbol	Pivot Price	Name	Symbol	Quantity	Price

"You should always compare a company's earnings per share to the same quarter a year earlier, not to the prior quarter, to avoid any distortion due to seasonality."

Stocks to Watch			Today's Trades			
Name	Symbol	Pivot Price	Name	Symbol	Quantity	Price

"Even if you sold out completely and moved entirely to cash, you never want to throw in the towel because bear markets create new bases on new stocks that could be the next cycle's 1,000% winners."

Stocks to Watch			Today's Trades			
Name	Symbol	Pivot Price	Name	Symbol	Quantity	Price

"Any time you see a one-time aberration in economic data that is reported once a month, you should not give it too much weight. One month does not make a trend. Four or five months of data would make a trend, but one month of data could be ignored."

Stocks to Watch			Today's Trades			
Name	Symbol	Pivot Price	Name	Symbol	Quantity	Price

"On May 23, 1995, home loan lender Aames Financial Corp. emerged from a nearly two-year-long, giant cup-with-handle base and initiated a 71-week move that took the stock up 567%."

Aames Financial Corp Weekly Chart   **1995**

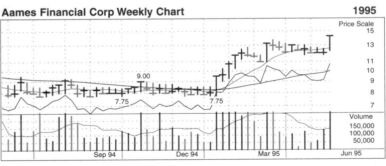

Stocks to Watch			Stocks to Watch		
Name	Symbol	Pivot Price	Name	Symbol	Pivot Price

MONDAY
24
MAY
2004

"When the market indexes close down on heavier volume, or if they appear to be flat or only slightly up on big volume (the appearance of churning), as long as the daily range remains tight the pattern is still considered to be constructive."

Stocks to Watch			Today's Trades			
Name	Symbol	Pivot Price	Name	Symbol	Quantity	Price

TUESDAY
25
MAY
2004

"Current quarterly earnings per share should be up a major percentage—at least 25% to 50% or more—over the same quarter in the previous year. The best companies might show earnings up 100% to 500% or more! When picking winning stocks, it's the bottom line that counts."

Stocks to Watch			Today's Trades			
Name	Symbol	Pivot Price	Name	Symbol	Quantity	Price

"Use sponsorship as your fundamental research–
ask yourself if the better funds own significant
positions in a stock. If so, then they have probably
done their homework and in the process confirm
your own homework."

Stocks to Watch			Today's Trades			
Name	Symbol	Pivot Price	Name	Symbol	Quantity	Price

"Four days of distribution, if correctly spotted over a two or
three week period, are often enough to turn a previously
advancing market into a decline."

Nasdaq Composite Daily Chart   **2000**

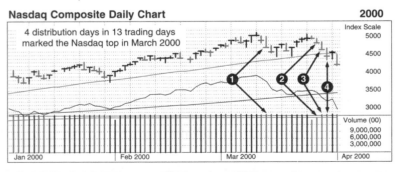

4 distribution days in 13 trading days
marked the Nasdaq top in March 2000

Stocks to Watch			Today's Trades			
Name	Symbol	Pivot Price	Name	Symbol	Quantity	Price

FRIDAY
28
MAY
2004

"Any stock that rises close to 20% should never be allowed to drop back into the loss column. If you made a mistake by not taking your profit, avoid making a second mistake and letting the position develop into a loss."

Stocks to Watch			Today's Trades			
Name	Symbol	Pivot Price	Name	Symbol	Quantity	Price

SAT/SUN
29/30
MAY
2004

"If you think of stocks as baseball players, you're going to want as many .300 hitters as possible on your team. They cost more than .200 hitters (these stocks that have higher P/Es) but you'll win more games."

Stocks to Watch			Stocks to Watch		
Name	Symbol	Pivot Price	Name	Symbol	Pivot Price

NOTES:

NOTES:

MONDAY

31

MAY

2004

"On this day in 1995, healthcare benefits administrator ABR Information Services came out of a very flat, nine-week base and over the next 51 weeks ran up a blistering 492%."

A B R Information Services Weekly Chart   1995

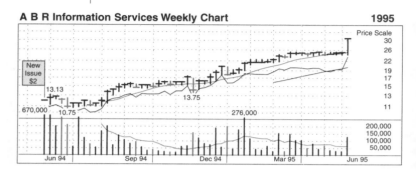

U.S. equity markets closed
in observance of Memorial Day.

TUESDAY

1

JUNE

2004

"A primary concept is to let the market tell you what to do and what stocks to buy. Look for where the money is flowing, and put money into stocks that are showing strength. Choose the stock that is moving over the one that isn't, because that alone is telling you something."

Stocks to Watch			Today's Trades			
Name	Symbol	Pivot Price	Name	Symbol	Quantity	Price

"Price projection of a true leader—Take the P/E at the first stage breakout and multiply by 130%. Take this number and then multiply it by the consensus estimate going out 2 years."

Stocks to Watch			Today's Trades			
Name	Symbol	Pivot Price	Name	Symbol	Quantity	Price

"Many big investors get out of a stock before trouble appears on the income statement. You buy with heavy emphasis on fundamentals and sell on unusual market action (price and volume movement)."

Stocks to Watch			Today's Trades			
Name	Symbol	Pivot Price	Name	Symbol	Quantity	Price

FRIDAY
4
JUNE
2004

"On this day in 1999, Checkpoint Software flew out of a 19-week cup-with-handle to ignite a massive 1,104% move in only 40 weeks."

Checkpoint Software Technologies Ltd Weekly Chart   **1999**

Stocks to Watch		
Name	Symbol	Pivot Price

Today's Trades			
Name	Symbol	Quantity	Price

SAT/SUN
5/6
JUNE
2004

"Use the IBD Mutual Fund Index to measure the strength or weakness of the market—when the individual points on the chart start showing a lot of upside or downside distance between points (e.g., steep moves) on a day-to-day basis, this can imply larger market moves in the same direction."

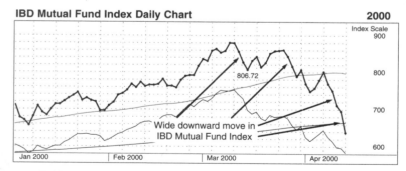

IBD Mutual Fund Index Daily Chart   **2000**

Stocks to Watch		
Name	Symbol	Pivot Price

Stocks to Watch		
Name	Symbol	Pivot Price

"Strong current quarterly earnings are not enough—to ensure the latest results aren't just a flash in the pan, look for annual earnings per share that have increased every year for the last three years."

Stocks to Watch			Today's Trades			
Name	Symbol	Pivot Price	Name	Symbol	Quantity	Price

"We found through research that almost all sound, short-selling patterns occur five to seven months after a formerly huge market leader has clearly topped."

Stocks to Watch			Today's Trades			
Name	Symbol	Pivot Price	Name	Symbol	Quantity	Price

"It takes big demand to move prices up, and by far the largest source of big demand for stocks is institutional investors who account for the lion's share of each day's market activity."

Stocks to Watch			Today's Trades			
Name	Symbol	Pivot Price	Name	Symbol	Quantity	Price

"It is important to watch trading volume as the market breaks to new lows—is it light, or heavy? If volume is light as the market undercuts prior lows, it may indicate that selling has exhausted itself."

Stocks to Watch			Today's Trades			
Name	Symbol	Pivot Price	Name	Symbol	Quantity	Price

FRIDAY
11
JUNE
2004

"Everything sells for about what it's worth at the time. If a company's price and P/E ratio change in the near future, it's because conditions, events, psychology, and earnings continue to improve or suddenly start to deteriorate as the weeks and months pass."

Stocks to Watch			Today's Trades			
Name	Symbol	Pivot Price	Name	Symbol	Quantity	Price

SAT/SUN
12/13
JUNE
2004

"Sometimes a stock's chart pattern can be influenced by sharp, wide movements in the broader market. Study a stock chart's price and volume relationships to determine when a stock is under accumulation—do not rely on how perfect or imperfect the shape of the chart base is."

Stocks to Watch			Stocks to Watch		
Name	Symbol	Pivot Price	Name	Symbol	Pivot Price

MONDAY
14
JUNE
2004

"Once the market puts in a follow-through buy signal and runs up for 13 weeks or so, it will then consolidate for the first time. This is normal, and you will get a sense of this as you run out of names to buy at logical points."

Stocks to Watch			Today's Trades			
Name	Symbol	Pivot Price	Name	Symbol	Quantity	Price

TUESDAY
15
JUNE
2004

"On this day in 1995, generic drug maker Dura Pharmaceuticals, shook out 'weak hands' before finding support at its 200-day moving average and bouncing out of an eight-week base to begin a 315% move over the next year."

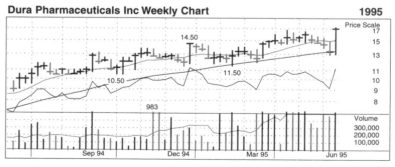

Dura Pharmaceuticals Inc Weekly Chart   **1995**

Stocks to Watch			Today's Trades			
Name	Symbol	Pivot Price	Name	Symbol	Quantity	Price

"Buying right vs. buying early: I always prefer to buy right!"

Stocks to Watch			Today's Trades			
Name	Symbol	Pivot Price	Name	Symbol	Quantity	Price

"While three out of four big market winners in the past were growth stocks, one in four was a turnaround situation."

Stocks to Watch			Today's Trades			
Name	Symbol	Pivot Price	Name	Symbol	Quantity	Price

"A flat base of five weeks or more is possible when a stock is in the middle of a big move, but for all other types of bases you would prefer to see 7-8 weeks or more."

Stocks to Watch			Today's Trades			
Name	Symbol	Pivot Price	Name	Symbol	Quantity	Price

"Buying stocks that are extended too far from a correct buy point will result in more sharp sell-offs in price that will shake you out of a stock."

Stocks to Watch			Stocks to Watch		
Name	Symbol	Pivot Price	Name	Symbol	Pivot Price

"Study where you are in the 'bull game.' Know which part of the bull cycles you are in—the beginning, middle or the end."

Stocks to Watch			Today's Trades			
Name	Symbol	Pivot Price	Name	Symbol	Quantity	Price

"Tight price action in the market indexes during an uptrend is constructive."

Stocks to Watch			Today's Trades			
Name	Symbol	Pivot Price	Name	Symbol	Quantity	Price

WEDNESDAY

23

JUNE
2004

"High P/E's that were great bargains—Xerox sold for 100 times earnings in 1960—before it advanced 3,300% in price (from a split-adjusted $5 to $170). America Online sold for over 100 times earnings before increasing 14,900% in November 1994 to its top in December 1999."

Stocks to Watch			Today's Trades			
Name	Symbol	Pivot Price	Name	Symbol	Quantity	Price

THURSDAY

24

JUNE
2004

"You won't do well in your investing if you insist on buying 'cheap stocks' in the hope of 'discovering' a winner. Hope never works in the market unless you start with a quality stock that's begun to build steam."

Stocks to Watch			Today's Trades			
Name	Symbol	Pivot Price	Name	Symbol	Quantity	Price

"Note new stock positions bought by institutions in the last quarter—significant new positions taken in the most recently reported period are generally more relevant than existing positions held for some time."

Stocks to Watch			Today's Trades			
Name	Symbol	Pivot Price	Name	Symbol	Quantity	Price

"It's a constructive sign when the number of weeks the stock closes up in price on above average weekly volume outnumber the number of weeks it closes down in price on above average volume while still forming its base."

Stocks to Watch			Stocks to Watch		
Name	Symbol	Pivot Price	Name	Symbol	Pivot Price

MONDAY
28
JUNE
2004

"If a stock's price is extended for many months and closes the day with a larger price increase than on any previous up days since the beginning of the whole move up, watch out! This usually occurs very close to a stock's peak, or top."

Qualcomm Inc Daily Chart　　　　　　　　　　　　　　**2000**

Biggest point gain of 39 points in entire move occurs 4 days before top.

Stocks to Watch		
Name	Symbol	Pivot Price

Today's Trades			
Name	Symbol	Quantity	Price

TUESDAY
29
JUNE
2004

"On June 19, 1994, technology research firm Gartner, riding the first wave of the 1990's computer/Internet boom, broke out of a 17-week cup-with-handle and staged its own boom, moving 667% higher over the next 68 weeks."

Gartner Inc Weekly Chart　　　　　　　　　　　　　　**1994**

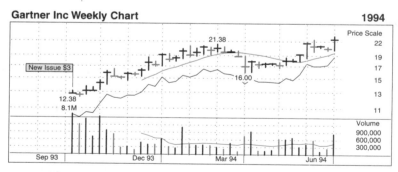

Stocks to Watch		
Name	Symbol	Pivot Price

Today's Trades			
Name	Symbol	Quantity	Price

"When the 'Investment Advisers Bullish/Bearish' indicator is at a high bullish level near the beginning of a bull move, it is more often a sign of strength than a contrarian indicator."

Stocks to Watch			Today's Trades			
Name	Symbol	Pivot Price	Name	Symbol	Quantity	Price

"In the beginning phase of a new bull market, growth stocks are usually the first to lead and make new price highs. Young growth stocks will usually dominate for at least two bull cycles. Basic industry groups such as steel, chemical, paper and machinery, and other so-called cyclical stocks usually lag."

Stocks to Watch			Today's Trades			
Name	Symbol	Pivot Price	Name	Symbol	Quantity	Price

NOTES:

NOTES:

"If some of the better-performing stock funds own large positions in a stock, then they will probably support the stock when it sells off a bit. This is a key concept when assessing the benefits of quality sponsorship in a stock."

Stocks to Watch			Today's Trades			
Name	Symbol	Pivot Price	Name	Symbol	Quantity	Price

"Institutional buying and selling account for more than 70% of the activity in most leading companies. This is the sustained force behind most important price moves."

Stocks to Watch			Stocks to Watch		
Name	Symbol	Pivot Price	Name	Symbol	Pivot Price

"It is the combination of strong earnings in the last few quarters plus a record of solid growth in recent years that creates a superb stock, or at least one with a higher probability for success."

U.S. equity markets closed in observance of Independence Day.

"In my opinion, it's usually better for a company to split its shares 2-for-1 or 3-for-2 than 3-for-1 or 5-for-1. Oversized splits create a substantially larger supply of stock."

Stocks to Watch			Today's Trades			
Name	Symbol	Pivot Price	Name	Symbol	Quantity	Price

WEDNESDAY

7

**JULY
2004**

"Don't sell a stock solely because it has a 'D' Accumulation/ Distribution rating. Sometimes a stock can get a D rating while it is in a base-building process."

Stocks to Watch		
Name	Symbol	Pivot Price

Today's Trades			
Name	Symbol	Quantity	Price

THURSDAY

8

**JULY
2004**

"On this day in 1997, web portal pioneer Yahoo! Corp. broke out of a 19-week cup-with-handle and then pulled back for two weeks before beginning a 130-week romp that took the stock up 7,449%. Yahoo!"

Yahoo! Corp Weekly Chart   **1997**

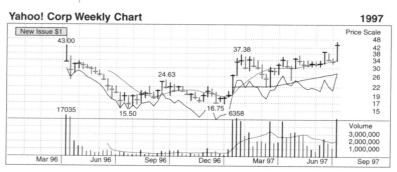

Stocks to Watch		
Name	Symbol	Pivot Price

Today's Trades			
Name	Symbol	Quantity	Price

FRIDAY

9

**JULY
2004**

"Oil stocks are essentially a commodity play and generally are not CAN SLIM growth situations. If you think the price of oil is going up, then buy oil stocks!"

Stocks to Watch			Today's Trades			
Name	Symbol	Pivot Price	Name	Symbol	Quantity	Price

SAT/SUN

10/11

**JULY
2004**

"Limit your use of limit orders. You never make big money in the stock market by eighths and quarters. Your objective should be to be right on the big moves, not the minor fluctuations."

Stocks to Watch			Stocks to Watch		
Name	Symbol	Pivot Price	Name	Symbol	Pivot Price

"On this day in 1965, semiconductor manufacturer Solitron Devices came out of a nine-week base and ran 578% over the next 41 weeks."

Solitron Devices Inc Weekly Chart   **1965**

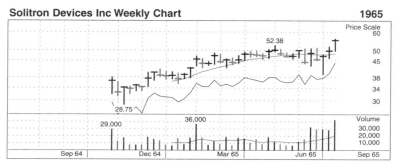

Stocks to Watch			**Today's Trades**			
Name	Symbol	Pivot Price	Name	Symbol	Quantity	Price

"Even if your stock is doing well, be wary if the overall industry group is underperforming the market. It could be a warning sign."

Stocks to Watch			**Today's Trades**			
Name	Symbol	Pivot Price	Name	Symbol	Quantity	Price

"Check the stability of a company's three year-earnings record and restrict your stock selections to ventures with proven growth records. Avoid stocks with erratic histories or cyclical recoveries in profits."

Stocks to Watch			Today's Trades			
Name	Symbol	Pivot Price	Name	Symbol	Quantity	Price

"Low mutual fund cash levels are not a problem—big funds can raise instant cash by selling one of their big laggards. They can sell 200,000 Dow Chemical here, 300,000 Dupont there, and get cash as they need it for stocks that are moving."

Stocks to Watch			Today's Trades			
Name	Symbol	Pivot Price	Name	Symbol	Quantity	Price

"The ultimate top in a stock might occur on the heaviest volume down day since the beginning of the stock's advance."

Stocks to Watch		
Name	Symbol	Pivot Price

Today's Trades			
Name	Symbol	Quantity	Price

"On July 17, 1998, Qlogic Corp. put on a huge volume display as it popped out of a 43-week cup-with-handle formation to begin a 3,120% trajectory over the next 86 weeks."

Qlogic Corp Weekly Chart
1998

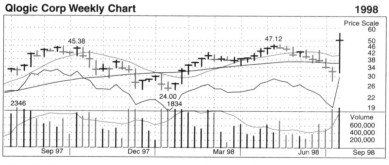

Stocks to Watch		
Name	Symbol	Pivot Price

Stocks to Watch		
Name	Symbol	Pivot Price

MONDAY
19
JULY
2004

"The annual rate of earnings growth in the companies you pick should be 25%, 50%, even 100% or more."

Stocks to Watch			Today's Trades			
Name	Symbol	Pivot Price	Name	Symbol	Quantity	Price

TUESDAY
20
JULY
2004

"Pivot buy points in correct chart patterns are not necessarily at a stock's old high. Most occur 5% to 10% below the former peak."

Stocks to Watch			Today's Trades			
Name	Symbol	Pivot Price	Name	Symbol	Quantity	Price

"In our study of the greatest stock market winners from 1952 through 2001 we discovered that more than 95% of the greatest successes met one or more of the following criteria: A rapidly selling new product or service, new management, new ideas, or a new high in its stock price."

Stocks to Watch			Today's Trades			
Name	Symbol	Pivot Price	Name	Symbol	Quantity	Price

THURSDAY

22

JULY
2004

"Use the scientific method and do what scientists do: Constantly ask where you are wrong. Correct where you are wrong and you will improve."

Stocks to Watch			Today's Trades			
Name	Symbol	Pivot Price	Name	Symbol	Quantity	Price

FRIDAY

23

**JULY
2004**

"On this day in 1963, Syntex Corp., makers of the birth-control pill, emerged from a high, tight flag formation and quickly ran up 488% over the next 25 weeks."

Syntex Corp Weekly Chart   **1963**

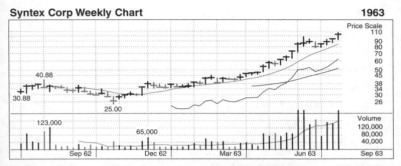

Stocks to Watch			Today's Trades			
Name	Symbol	Pivot Price	Name	Symbol	Quantity	Price

SAT/SUN

24/25

**JULY
2004**

"You can be right on every factor concerning an individual stock, but if you are wrong about the direction of the general market, three out of four of your stocks will plummet with the market averages and you will certainly lose money big time."

Stocks to Watch			Stocks to Watch		
Name	Symbol	Pivot Price	Name	Symbol	Pivot Price

MONDAY

26

JULY
2004

"Jesse Livermore said, 'You fear when you should hope, and you hope when you should fear.' Are you fearing, or are you hoping?"

Stocks to Watch			Today's Trades			
Name	Symbol	Pivot Price	Name	Symbol	Quantity	Price

TUESDAY

27

JULY
2004

"IQ and education mean nothing in the stock market. Don't let your presumed intelligence get in the way of making money in stocks."

Stocks to Watch			Today's Trades			
Name	Symbol	Pivot Price	Name	Symbol	Quantity	Price

WEDNESDAY

28

JULY
2004

"All stocks are bad—unless they go higher in price!"

Stocks to Watch			Today's Trades			
Name	Symbol	Pivot Price	Name	Symbol	Quantity	Price

THURSDAY

29

JULY
2004

"Day-to-day news items are overemphasized. Stick to your methods and let the market's own action be your guide."

Stocks to Watch			Today's Trades			
Name	Symbol	Pivot Price	Name	Symbol	Quantity	Price

NOTES:

NOTES:

"Between 1980 and 2000, the median annual growth rate of all outstanding stocks in our study at their early emerging stage was 36%."

Stocks to Watch			Today's Trades			
Name	Symbol	Pivot Price	Name	Symbol	Quantity	Price

"The more desirable growth stocks normally correct 1½ to 2½ times the general market averages. In a bull market correction, growth stocks declining the least are usually your best selections. The stocks that drop the most are normally your weakest."

Stocks to Watch			Stocks to Watch		
Name	Symbol	Pivot Price	Name	Symbol	Pivot Price

MONDAY

2

AUGUST

2004

"On this day in 1994, IPO Ascend Communications, developers of a back-bone networking technology known as asynchronous transfer mode, shook out weak holders in its initial six-week base before rocketing 3,253% over the next 94 weeks."

Ascend Communications Inc Weekly Chart   **1994**

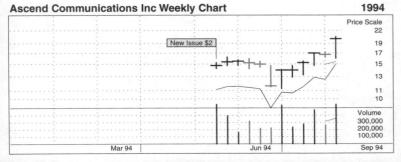

Stocks to Watch			Today's Trades			
<u>Name</u>	<u>Symbol</u>	<u>Pivot Price</u>	<u>Name</u>	<u>Symbol</u>	<u>Quantity</u>	<u>Price</u>

TUESDAY

3

AUGUST

2004

"Unlike some institutional investors who may be restricted by the size of their funds, individual investors have the luxury of investing in only the very best stocks in each bull cycle."

Stocks to Watch			Today's Trades			
<u>Name</u>	<u>Symbol</u>	<u>Pivot Price</u>	<u>Name</u>	<u>Symbol</u>	<u>Quantity</u>	<u>Price</u>

"If you owned a store that sold red and yellow dresses, and nobody bought the yellow dresses, would you add yellow dresses to your store's inventory? Of course not! The same goes for stocks—add to your winners and cut your losers."

Stocks to Watch			Today's Trades			
Name	Symbol	Pivot Price	Name	Symbol	Quantity	Price

"If you do consider options, you should limit the percentage of your total portfolio committed to them. A prudent limit is 10% to 15%."

Stocks to Watch			Today's Trades			
Name	Symbol	Pivot Price	Name	Symbol	Quantity	Price

FRIDAY
6
AUGUST
2004

"There is absolutely no good reason for a stock to go anywhere in a big, sustainable way if current earnings are poor."

Stocks to Watch			Today's Trades			
Name	Symbol	Pivot Price	Name	Symbol	Quantity	Price

SAT/SUN
7/8
AUGUST
2004

"On August 7, 1979, Wal Mart Stores, taking the retail warehouse concept to a new level, emerged from a 43-week cup-with-handle base and gained 7,250% over the next 8 years!"

Wal Mart Stores Weekly Chart   **1979**

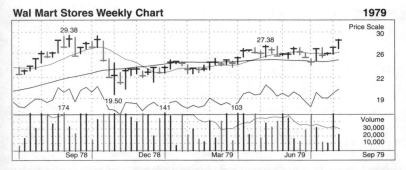

Stocks to Watch			Stocks to Watch		
Name	Symbol	Pivot Price	Name	Symbol	Pivot Price

MONDAY
9
AUGUST
2004

"Keep your head in a bull market and don't lose perspective! When everyone is euphoric and having visions of yachts and fancy cars, it may be time to sell."

Stocks to Watch		
Name	Symbol	Pivot Price

Today's Trades			
Name	Symbol	Quantity	Price

TUESDAY
10
AUGUST
2004

"On this day in 1994, PeopleSoft emerged from a 21-month cup-with-handle base and went on a 45-month romp that carried the stock to a more than 2,100% gain."

PeopleSoft Weekly Chart   1994

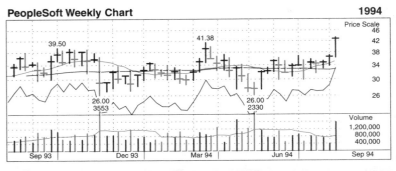

Stocks to Watch		
Name	Symbol	Pivot Price

Today's Trades			
Name	Symbol	Quantity	Price

WEDNESDAY

11

AUGUST
2004

"Professional investors wield huge influence over
a stock's price. Thus, it's essential to buy the
better stocks that mutual funds are buying and
sell what they are selling on a heavy basis. A
quick way to keep track of professional trading is
to use the Accumulation/Distribution Rating."

Stocks to Watch			Today's Trades			
Name	Symbol	Pivot Price	Name	Symbol	Quantity	Price

THURSDAY

12

AUGUST
2004

"The second most important indicator of primary
changes in the market direction after the daily
averages is the way leading stocks act. If the
market leadership begins to falter, then so will
the market."

Stocks to Watch			Today's Trades			
Name	Symbol	Pivot Price	Name	Symbol	Quantity	Price

FRIDAY

13

AUGUST
2004

"If a stock that has been advancing rapidly is greatly extended from its original base many months ago and then opens on a gap up in price from the previous day's close, the advance is near its peak. This is called an exhaustion gap."

Ariba Inc Daily Chart

2000

Exhaustion gap occurs 4 days before final top.

SAT/SUN

14/15

AUGUST
2004

"On August 14, 1958, the dawning of the Space Age was upon us, and rocket fuel manufacturer Thiokol Chemical launched from a 25-week flat base to rocket 379% over the next 38 weeks."

Thiokol Chemical Corp Weekly Chart

1958

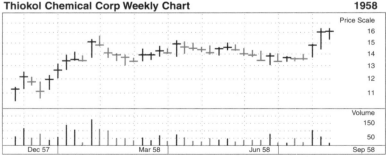

"With respect to annual earnings growth rates, you might accept one down year in the last five as long as the following year's earnings quickly recover and move back to new high ground."

Stocks to Watch			Today's Trades			
Name	Symbol	Pivot Price	Name	Symbol	Quantity	Price
_____	_____	_____	_____	_____	_____	_____
_____	_____	_____	_____	_____	_____	_____
_____	_____	_____	_____	_____	_____	_____

"A winning stock doesn't need a huge number of institutional owners, but it should have at least several. Ten might be a minimum reasonable number of institutional sponsors, although most stocks have a good many more."

Stocks to Watch			Today's Trades			
Name	Symbol	Pivot Price	Name	Symbol	Quantity	Price
_____	_____	_____	_____	_____	_____	_____
_____	_____	_____	_____	_____	_____	_____
_____	_____	_____	_____	_____	_____	_____

WEDNESDAY
18
AUGUST
2004

"If you buy more than 5% to 10% past the precise buy point, you are buying late and more than likely, you will get caught in the next price correction."

Stocks to Watch			Today's Trades			
Name	Symbol	Pivot Price	Name	Symbol	Quantity	Price

THURSDAY
19
AUGUST
2004

"Don't short an advancing stock just because its price seems too high."

Stocks to Watch			Today's Trades			
Name	Symbol	Pivot Price	Name	Symbol	Quantity	Price

"The unwillingness of investors to set and follow minimum standards for stock selection reminds me of doctors years ago who were ignorant of the need to sterilize their instruments before each operation."

Stocks to Watch			Today's Trades			
Name	Symbol	Pivot Price	Name	Symbol	Quantity	Price

"Major changes in volume can give you significant clues. A stock that trades up one point on 600% of its average volume alerts you to emerging professional interest in the stock."

Stocks to Watch			Stocks to Watch		
Name	Symbol	Pivot Price	Name	Symbol	Pivot Price

"A P/E ratio is more an indicator of how much investors value a company's earnings stream and not so much an indicator of the 'absolute' value of a stock. Oftentimes a company has a high P/E because investors place a high value on the quality of the earnings stream of that company."

Stocks to Watch			Today's Trades			
Name	Symbol	Pivot Price	Name	Symbol	Quantity	Price

"There are only two things you can really do when a new bear market begins: sell and get out or go short."

Stocks to Watch			Today's Trades			
Name	Symbol	Pivot Price	Name	Symbol	Quantity	Price

WEDNESDAY

25

AUGUST
2004

"Earnings per share of companies with high debt-to-equity ratios could be clobbered in difficult periods of high interest rates if they are constant issuers of debt. These highly leveraged companies are generally of lower quality and higher risk."

Stocks to Watch			Today's Trades			
Name	Symbol	Pivot Price	Name	Symbol	Quantity	Price

THURSDAY

26

AUGUST
2004

"Our studies show that the greatest winning stocks of the past 50 years had a return on equity (ROE) of at least 17%. Return on equity helps separate the well-managed companies from the poorly managed ones."

Stocks to Watch			Today's Trades			
Name	Symbol	Pivot Price	Name	Symbol	Quantity	Price

"Learn to read weekly charts as they will help you gauge institutional buying. Institutions can take days, if not weeks, to build or unload their positions, so heavy volume on a weekly chart may tell you if they're possibly moving in or out of a stock in a big way."

Stocks to Watch			Today's Trades			
Name	Symbol	Pivot Price	Name	Symbol	Quantity	Price

"On August 28, 1965, Admiral Corporation, bringing color television to the masses, catapulted out of a 14-week cup-with-handle base and set out on a 312% upside move for the next 34 weeks."

Admiral Corp Weekly Chart   **1965**

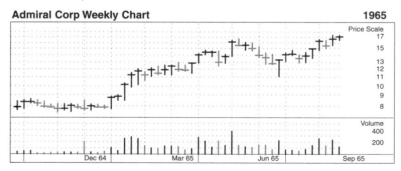

Stocks to Watch			Stocks to Watch		
Name	Symbol	Pivot Price	Name	Symbol	Pivot Price

"Sometimes the 'ego indicator' can tell you when a stock may be on its last legs. When management begins to buy expensive office space, furniture, artwork, luxury homes and cars, etc., it may be a sign that its focus is no longer on the business. When this occurs, watch out!"

Stocks to Watch			Today's Trades			
Name	Symbol	Pivot Price	Name	Symbol	Quantity	Price

"Cup patterns can last from seven to as long as 65 weeks, but most are three to six months."

Stocks to Watch			Today's Trades			
Name	Symbol	Pivot Price	Name	Symbol	Quantity	Price

NOTES:

NOTES:

"If you are choosing between two stocks to buy, one with 5 billion shares outstanding and the other with 50 million, the smaller one will usually be the better performer, if other factors are equal. However since smaller-cap stocks are less liquid, they come down as fast as they go up, sometimes even faster."

Stocks to Watch			Today's Trades			
Name	Symbol	Pivot Price	Name	Symbol	Quantity	Price

"What is an investor to do in a bear market? Study, study, study your past mistakes, sharpen your investment skills, and get ready for the next bull market."

Stocks to Watch			Today's Trades			
Name	Symbol	Pivot Price	Name	Symbol	Quantity	Price

"A stock will often top in price around the second or third time it splits. Our study of the biggest winners found only 18% of them had splits in the year preceding their great price advances."

Stocks to Watch			Today's Trades			
Name	Symbol	Pivot Price	Name	Symbol	Quantity	Price

"What is the main characteristic of a successful person? A successful person has a habit of doing what failures don't want to do: work hard, do their homework, and go the extra mile."

Stocks to Watch			Stocks to Watch		
Name	Symbol	Pivot Price	Name	Symbol	Pivot Price

MONDAY

6

SEPTEMBER
2004

"'Railroad tracks' occur when a stock retraces the prior week's price spread from the prior week's low to its high point and closes the week up a little, with volume remaining very high. These two parallel vertical lines on a weekly chart indicate heavy volume distribution without real additional price progress for the week."

Kulicke & Soffa Inds Inc Weekly Chart   **1995**

U.S. equity markets closed in observance of Labor Day.

TUESDAY

7

SEPTEMBER
2004

"You live in a fantastic time of unlimited opportunity, an era of outstanding new ideas, emerging industries, and new frontiers."

Stocks to Watch			Today's Trades			
Name	Symbol	Pivot Price	Name	Symbol	Quantity	Price

"On this day in 1997, Amazon.com, pioneering a new era of online shopping, burst out of a 17-week cup-with-handle base and lifted 1,539% in only 16 weeks."

Amazon.com Inc Weekly Chart   **1997**

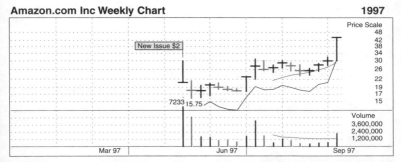

Stocks to Watch			Today's Trades			
Name	Symbol	Pivot Price	Name	Symbol	Quantity	Price

"On this date in 1999, the buzz was 'B2B' or business-to-business online commerce, and B2B pioneer Commerce One flew out of a narrow, v-shaped, 10-week cup-with-handle-type base to log a 1,539% gain in a mere 16 weeks."

Commerce One Inc Weekly Chart   **1999**

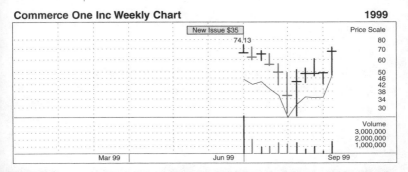

Stocks to Watch			Today's Trades			
Name	Symbol	Pivot Price	Name	Symbol	Quantity	Price

"Our market studies showed that 97% of all the greatest Nasdaq stocks broke out of their initial sound chart patterns at prices of $15 and higher and NYSE stocks at $20 and higher."

Stocks to Watch			Today's Trades			
Name	Symbol	Pivot Price	Name	Symbol	Quantity	Price

"Remember consensus earnings estimates are opinions and opinions may be wrong. Actual reported earnings are facts."

Stocks to Watch			Stocks to Watch		
Name	Symbol	Pivot Price	Name	Symbol	Pivot Price

"In one of our model book studies performed in 1995, we found that the median correction for big leaders in one cycle was 72% off the absolute top. Sixty percent of the leaders were able to come out of their correction, but it took an average of four years to do so if the correction was 50% or less. The moral: look for new leaders, the 'new merchandise' in any new bull cycle."

Stocks to Watch			Today's Trades			
Name	Symbol	Pivot Price	Name	Symbol	Quantity	Price

"Some stocks may be sold when they are 70% to 100% or more above their 200-day moving average price line."

Stocks to Watch			Today's Trades			
Name	Symbol	Pivot Price	Name	Symbol	Quantity	Price

WEDNESDAY
15
SEPTEMBER
2004

"On this day in 1970, Levitz Furniture broke out of a 34-week cup-with-handle base and began a 242% run that lasted 49 weeks."

Levitz Furniture Corp Weekly Chart — **1970**

Stocks to Watch			Today's Trades			
Name	Symbol	Pivot Price	Name	Symbol	Quantity	Price

THURSDAY
16
SEPTEMBER
2004

"Unless you travel a lot and are unable to watch your stocks closely, it's usually better not to enter stop-loss orders. In doing so, you and other similarly minded investors are showing your hand to the market makers. At times, they might drop the stock to shakeout stop-loss orders."

Stocks to Watch			Today's Trades			
Name	Symbol	Pivot Price	Name	Symbol	Quantity	Price

"When a stock forms a proper cup-with-handle chart pattern and then charges through the pivot point, the day's volume should increase at least 50% above normal."

Stocks to Watch			Today's Trades			
Name	Symbol	Pivot Price	Name	Symbol	Quantity	Price
_____	_____	_____	_____	_____	_____	_____
_____	_____	_____	_____	_____	_____	_____
_____	_____	_____	_____	_____	_____	_____

"In our models of the 600 best-performing stocks from 1952 to 2001, three out of four showed earnings increases averaging more than 70% in the latest publicly recorded quarter before they began their major advances."

Stocks to Watch			Stocks to Watch		
Name	Symbol	Pivot Price	Name	Symbol	Pivot Price
_____	_____	_____	_____	_____	_____
_____	_____	_____	_____	_____	_____
_____	_____	_____	_____	_____	_____

"Analyze the way the market reacts to general news. If highly positive news hits the market and stocks give ground slightly, the tape analyst might conclude the underpinnings of the market are weaker than previously believed."

Stocks to Watch			Today's Trades			
Name	Symbol	Pivot Price	Name	Symbol	Quantity	Price
___	___	___	___	___	___	___
___	___	___	___	___	___	___
___	___	___	___	___	___	___

"Investors make too much out of Federal budget deficits. The country may incur a budget deficit, but that implies that an asset is held somewhere to balance that deficit. Deficits are not black holes—somewhere there is an asset balancing against the deficit."

Stocks to Watch			Today's Trades			
Name	Symbol	Pivot Price	Name	Symbol	Quantity	Price
___	___	___	___	___	___	___
___	___	___	___	___	___	___
___	___	___	___	___	___	___

"'Distribution days' in the market indices that occur on less than average daily volume might argue more for a back-and-forth type of market instead of a general market decline."

Stocks to Watch			Today's Trades			
Name	Symbol	Pivot Price	Name	Symbol	Quantity	Price

THURSDAY

23

SEPTEMBER
2004

"The usual correction from the absolute peak (from the top of the cup) to the low point (bottom of the cup) of most price patterns varies from around the 12% to 15% range to upwards of 33%."

Ryland Group Inc Weekly Chart   **2001**

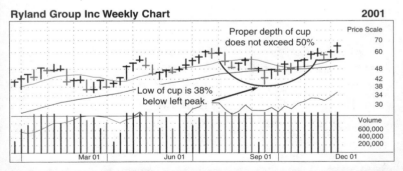

Stocks to Watch			Today's Trades			
Name	Symbol	Pivot Price	Name	Symbol	Quantity	Price

"When a stock with all the proper CAN SLIM characteristics breaks out powerfully from a base and moves up rapidly, in general you can add to your position on the first pullback to the 50-day moving average."

Cobra Golf Inc Weekly Chart   **1994**

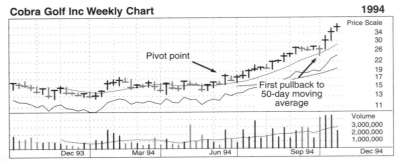

Stocks to Watch		
Name	Symbol	Pivot Price

Today's Trades			
Name	Symbol	Quantity	Price

"Bull and bear markets don't end easily. After everyone who can be run in or run out has thrown in the towel, there isn't anyone left to take action in the same direction. The market will finally turn and begin a whole new trend."

Stocks to Watch		
Name	Symbol	Pivot Price

Stocks to Watch		
Name	Symbol	Pivot Price

MONDAY
27
SEPTEMBER
2004

"A stock that shows three weekly closes in a row that are very close together is showing what I call 'three weeks tight,' which is generally a positive chart formation for a stock."

Verisign Inc Weekly Chart   **1999**

Stocks to Watch			Today's Trades			
Name	Symbol	Pivot Price	Name	Symbol	Quantity	Price

TUESDAY
28
SEPTEMBER
2004

"After a long advance, heavy daily volume without further upside price progress signals distribution. Sell your stock before the unsuspecting buyers are overwhelmed."

Stocks to Watch			Today's Trades			
Name	Symbol	Pivot Price	Name	Symbol	Quantity	Price

NOTES:

NOTES:

"If a stock has no professional sponsorship, chances are that its performance will be more run-of-the-mill. Odds are that at least several of the more than a thousand institutional investors have looked at the stock and passed it over."

Stocks to Watch			Today's Trades			
Name	Symbol	Pivot Price	Name	Symbol	Quantity	Price

"There should be some tight areas (small price variation from high to low for the week) in the price patterns of stocks under accumulation."

Stocks to Watch			Today's Trades			
Name	Symbol	Pivot Price	Name	Symbol	Quantity	Price

"Search for companies that have developed
important new products or services, or benefited
from new management or new industry
conditions. Then buy their stocks when they are
emerging from price consolidation patterns and
are close to, or actually making, new price highs."

Stocks to Watch			Today's Trades			
Name	Symbol	Pivot Price	Name	Symbol	Quantity	Price

"Your objective in the market is to make big
money when you are right."

Stocks to Watch			Stocks to Watch		
Name	Symbol	Pivot Price	Name	Symbol	Pivot Price

"If your stock is up 20% from its pivot point in only 1, 2 or 3 weeks, then be certain to hold the stock through its first 20 to 25% correction as well as a minimum of eight weeks."

Stocks to Watch			Today's Trades			
Name	Symbol	Pivot Price	Name	Symbol	Quantity	Price

"Shifts in market direction can also be detected by reviewing the last four or five stock purchases in your own portfolio. If you haven't made a dime on any of them, you could be picking up signs of a new downtrend."

Stocks to Watch			Today's Trades			
Name	Symbol	Pivot Price	Name	Symbol	Quantity	Price

"Our studies have concluded that the stocks you select should show a major percentage increase in current quarterly earnings per share when compared to the prior year's same quarter."

Stocks to Watch			Today's Trades			
Name	Symbol	Pivot Price	Name	Symbol	Quantity	Price

"To really do well in stocks, you simply have to know how to interpret the direction of the daily general market averages. Learn to recognize variations on a day-to-day basis. As you start to review market action on a daily basis, you'll begin to recognize the key signs of emerging new trends."

Stocks to Watch			Today's Trades			
Name	Symbol	Pivot Price	Name	Symbol	Quantity	Price

FRIDAY

8

OCTOBER
2004

"Selling short can be profitable, but it's a very difficult and highly specialized skill that should only be attempted in bear markets. But be forewarned: Few people make money shorting."

Stocks to Watch				Today's Trades			
Name	Symbol	Pivot Price		Name	Symbol	Quantity	Price

SAT/SUN

9/10

OCTOBER
2004

"The market frequently shows its true colors in the last hour of the day, either coming on and closing strong, or suddenly weakening and failing to hold gains established early in the session."

Stocks to Watch				Stocks to Watch		
Name	Symbol	Pivot Price		Name	Symbol	Pivot Price

MONDAY
11
OCTOBER
2004

"Investors who can be right and sit tight are uncommon. Learn to know what you own and how to handle it so you can make big money and capitalize on your best selection."

Stocks to Watch			Today's Trades			
Name	Symbol	Pivot Price	Name	Symbol	Quantity	Price

TUESDAY
12
OCTOBER
2004

"Bear markets usually end when business is still in a downtrend. Bull markets usually top out and turn down before a recession sets in. For this reason, use of economic indicators to tell you when to buy or sell stocks is not recommended."

Stocks to Watch			Today's Trades			
Name	Symbol	Pivot Price	Name	Symbol	Quantity	Price

WEDNESDAY
13
OCTOBER
2004

"A strong price pattern of any type should always have a clear and definite uptrend prior to the beginning of its base pattern. You should look for at least a 30% increase in price in the prior uptrend."

Stocks to Watch			Today's Trades			
Name	Symbol	Pivot Price	Name	Symbol	Quantity	Price

THURSDAY
14
OCTOBER
2004

"Once a general-market decline is over, the first stocks that bounce back to new price highs are almost always your authentic leaders. These breakouts continue week by week for about three months."

Stocks to Watch			Today's Trades			
Name	Symbol	Pivot Price	Name	Symbol	Quantity	Price

"As soon as a stock reports its third quarter in a row of accelerating earnings and accelerating sales, you can generally go right in and buy the stock regardless of whether or not it is extended from its nearest base."

Stocks to Watch			Today's Trades			
Name	Symbol	Pivot Price	Name	Symbol	Quantity	Price

"Buy from among the best two or three stocks in a group. The top two or three stocks in an industry group can have unbelievable growth, while others in the pack may hardly stir."

Stocks to Watch			Stocks to Watch		
Name	Symbol	Pivot Price	Name	Symbol	Pivot Price

"Studies show that 37% of a stock's price movement is tied to the performance of the industry group the stock is in. Another 12% is due to the strength in its overall sector. It is critical to consider a stock's industry group before making a purchase."

Stocks to Watch			Today's Trades			
Name	Symbol	Pivot Price	Name	Symbol	Quantity	Price

"On this day in 1990, Cisco Systems gapped up out of its base on huge volume and began a 1,938% run over the next 41 months."

Cisco Systems Inc Weekly Chart   1990

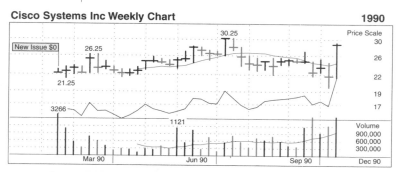

Stocks to Watch			Today's Trades			
Name	Symbol	Pivot Price	Name	Symbol	Quantity	Price

WEDNESDAY
20
OCTOBER
2004

"In most, but not all, cases, the bottom part of the cup in a cup-with-handle pattern should be rounded and give the appearance of a 'U' rather than a very narrow 'V'."

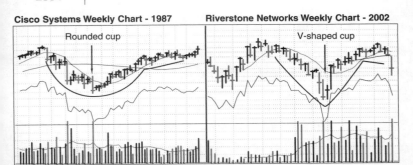

Cisco Systems Weekly Chart - 1987   **Riverstone Networks Weekly Chart - 2002**

Rounded cup   V-shaped cup

Stocks to Watch		
Name	Symbol	Pivot Price

Today's Trades			
Name	Symbol	Quantity	Price

THURSDAY
21
OCTOBER
2004

"Stocks tend to top around excessive stock splits. Sell if a stock runs up 25% to 50% for one or two weeks on a stock split."

Stocks to Watch		
Name	Symbol	Pivot Price

Today's Trades			
Name	Symbol	Quantity	Price

FRIDAY
22
OCTOBER
2004

"A secret to staying in a big winner: once a CAN SLIM stock is up and out of its base and moving sharply higher, expand the eight-week rule and try to stay with it for a minimum of 26 weeks. This will keep you in through the first good-sized correction and enable you to capitalize on a potential huge winner."

Stocks to Watch			Today's Trades			
Name	Symbol	Pivot Price	Name	Symbol	Quantity	Price

SAT/SUN
23/24
OCTOBER
2004

"Don't let anyone tell you that you can't time the market."

Stocks to Watch			Stocks to Watch		
Name	Symbol	Pivot Price	Name	Symbol	Pivot Price

"The stock market is the only thing in life that is
"the great leveler." You can argue with your
spouse, your family, your co-workers, etc., but you
can't argue with the market because it will clean
you out—it doesn't care who you are!"

Stocks to Watch			Today's Trades			
Name	Symbol	Pivot Price	Name	Symbol	Quantity	Price

"On this day in 1998, online auctioneer and new issue eBay
emerged from a very short 4-week 'cup' and catapulted
857% over the next 26 weeks."

Ebay Inc Weekly Chart   **1998**

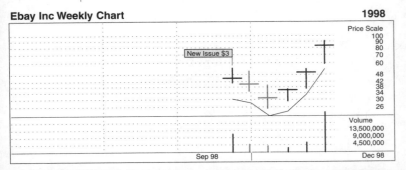

Stocks to Watch			Today's Trades			
Name	Symbol	Pivot Price	Name	Symbol	Quantity	Price

WEDNESDAY

27

OCTOBER
2004

"Bringing the Internet to the masses, America Online heralded the Internet boom by breaking out of an eight-week cup-with-handle base on this day in 1998 and setting the stage for a 67-week, 1,460% price gain."

America Online Inc Weekly Chart   **1998**

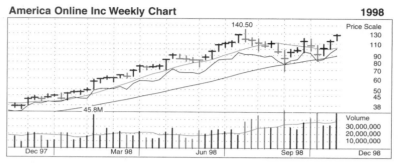

Stocks to Watch			Today's Trades			
Name	Symbol	Pivot Price	Name	Symbol	Quantity	Price

THURSDAY

28

OCTOBER
2004

"After a severe bear market, it is not critical for the public to come back into the market to start a new bull. It is important, however, that *institutions* come back into the market."

Stocks to Watch			Today's Trades			
Name	Symbol	Pivot Price	Name	Symbol	Quantity	Price

"Of all the studies done on the common characteristics that big winners share, none stood out as boldly as the latest quarter or two of profits each big winner reported just prior to its major price advance."

Stocks to Watch			Today's Trades			
Name	Symbol	Pivot Price	Name	Symbol	Quantity	Price

"If you come across a CAN SLIM stock that has formed three base on bases during a poor market period, creating a 'stairstep' look to its chart pattern, odds are that stock will become a powerful new leader. Once the weight of the market is lifted by a turn to the upside, such stocks can have a huge moves. I call this an 'ascending base.'"

America Online Inc Weekly Chart   **1999**

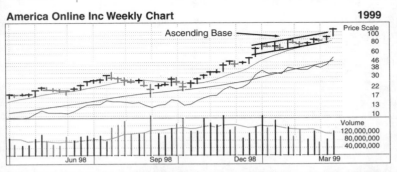

Stocks to Watch			Stocks to Watch		
Name	Symbol	Pivot Price	Name	Symbol	Pivot Price

NOTES:

NOTES:

MONDAY
1
NOVEMBER
2004

"On this day in 1962, Chrysler Corporation emerged from a 36-week cup-with-handle base from which it launched on a one-year, 242% run."

Chrysler Corp Weekly Chart   **1962**

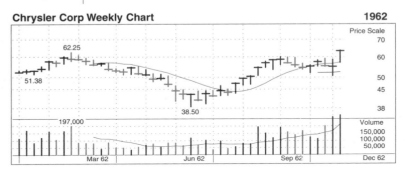

Stocks to Watch			Today's Trades			
Name	Symbol	Pivot Price	Name	Symbol	Quantity	Price

TUESDAY
2
NOVEMBER
2004

"Studying market history and precedent is key to understanding the market, but since most people tend to grasp onto what is the hot fad right now, this is overlooked. Their mentality is not oriented towards studying the past and they miss it when it repeats itself!"

Stocks to Watch			Today's Trades			
Name	Symbol	Pivot Price	Name	Symbol	Quantity	Price

"Beware of success that feeds your ego—if you get carried away with your success and allow a bloated sense of self-importance to overcome you, it is easy to forget what made you successful in the first place: hard work, constant study and self-review, and correction of your mistakes."

Stocks to Watch			Today's Trades			
Name	Symbol	Pivot Price	Name	Symbol	Quantity	Price

"Recognizing when the market has hit a top or has bottomed out is frequently 50% of the whole complicated ballgame. It's also the key investing skill virtually all amateur and professional investors alike seem to lack."

Stocks to Watch			Today's Trades			
Name	Symbol	Pivot Price	Name	Symbol	Quantity	Price

FRIDAY
5
NOVEMBER
2004

"On this day in 1986, Compaq Computer emerged from a 5½ month cup-with-handle base at $17 a share and over the next 11 months rose to a high of over $78 a share."

Compaq Computer Corp Weekly Chart   **1986**

Stocks to Watch			Today's Trades			
Name	Symbol	Pivot Price	Name	Symbol	Quantity	Price

SAT/SUN
6/7
NOVEMBER
2004

"Besides providing a framework for selecting winning stocks, CAN SLIM is also a 'market feedback' system, e.g., if CAN SLIM stocks are breaking out and failing, or if the rules of CAN SLIM suddenly seem like they 'don't work' anymore—that is telling you something about the health of the market."

Stocks to Watch			Stocks to Watch		
Name	Symbol	Pivot Price	Name	Symbol	Pivot Price

MONDAY

8

NOVEMBER

2004

"Analysis has shown that, on average, stocks in the top 50 or 100 groups perform better than those in the bottom 100. To increase your odds of finding a truly outstanding stock in an outstanding industry, concentrate on the top 40 groups."

Stocks to Watch			Today's Trades			
Name	Symbol	Pivot Price	Name	Symbol	Quantity	Price

TUESDAY

9

NOVEMBER

2004

"On this day in 1998, broadband semiconductor technology creator Broadcom began to move out of a jagged, 18-week double-bottom with handle chart base, setting the stage for a subsequent 71-week, 994% rally."

Broadcom Corp Weekly Chart 1998

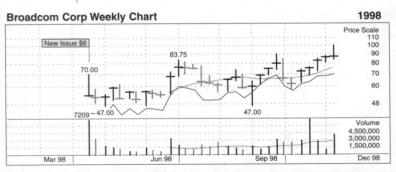

Stocks to Watch			Today's Trades			
Name	Symbol	Pivot Price	Name	Symbol	Quantity	Price

"Don't worry about sentiment indicators early in a bull market—they can mislead you."

Stocks to Watch			Today's Trades			
Name	Symbol	Pivot Price	Name	Symbol	Quantity	Price

"On this day in 1998, Applied Micro Circuits came out of a 28-week double-bottom chart formation to stage a 'macro' rally of 2,005% over the next 72 weeks"

Applied Micro Circuits Weekly Chart   **1998**

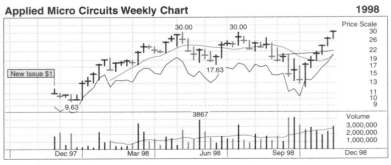

Stocks to Watch			Today's Trades			
Name	Symbol	Pivot Price	Name	Symbol	Quantity	Price

"After a big bull market ends, only one out of three tech leaders will get back to their old highs—the other two may never see the light of day again."

"On November 14, 1966, Monogram Industries, a manufacturer of self-contained toilets for airliners, spent 17 weeks building a base that flushed out weak holders by putting in three bottoms within the base before plumbing its way 909% higher over the next 57 weeks."

Monogram Industries Inc Weekly Chart   **1966**

"Most big, winning stocks last 10-14 months, on average, before they top."

Stocks to Watch			Today's Trades			
Name	Symbol	Pivot Price	Name	Symbol	Quantity	Price

"You should buy the really great companies—the ones that lead their industries and are number one in their particular field. All of my best big winners were the number one companies in their industries at the time they were purchased."

Stocks to Watch			Today's Trades			
Name	Symbol	Pivot Price	Name	Symbol	Quantity	Price

"A sign of a stock topping is when you observe a pattern of four or five down days followed by two or three up days whereas before the pattern would have been four or five up days followed by two or three down days."

Stocks to Watch			Today's Trades			
Name	Symbol	Pivot Price	Name	Symbol	Quantity	Price

"Watch the last forty minutes of the trading day during a bear market. Institutions may try to phony up a follow-through day by 'gunning' the market into the close. This type of phony rally in a bear market can only be mustered at the end of the day because it could not sustain itself if it had started earlier in the market day."

Stocks to Watch			Today's Trades			
Name	Symbol	Pivot Price	Name	Symbol	Quantity	Price

FRIDAY
19
NOVEMBER
2004

"The concept that the best time to short a former
leading stock is four to five months after the top is
simply the mirror image of what a stock looks like
when we consider it a buy. Just as we do not buy
a stock right off of its bottom, we don't short a
stock right off of its top! In both case, we let the
pattern develop first."

Stocks to Watch			Today's Trades			
Name	Symbol	Pivot Price	Name	Symbol	Quantity	Price

SAT/SUN
20/21
NOVEMBER
2004

"After the market has corrected 6-8 weeks or so
and former leaders that have held up well during
the correction start to get sold off, it often signals
the end of the correction. However, if leading
stocks begin to sell off before the correction has
put in a good 6-8 weeks, it may signal further
market weakness."

Stocks to Watch			Stocks to Watch		
Name	Symbol	Pivot Price	Name	Symbol	Pivot Price

"The law of supply and demand determines the price of almost everything in your daily life. This also applies to the stock market where it's more important than all the analysts' opinions on Wall Street."

Stocks to Watch			Today's Trades			
Name	Symbol	Pivot Price	Name	Symbol	Quantity	Price

"Shrewd investors should be aware of demographic trends. From data such as the number of people in various age groups, it's possible to predict potential growth for certain industries."

Stocks to Watch			Today's Trades			
Name	Symbol	Pivot Price	Name	Symbol	Quantity	Price

"When top-notch stocks are no longer leading the market up and cheap and lower-quality laggards are moving to the fore—these are warning signs that all is not right in the market, and a sharp correction might be just around the corner."

Stocks to Watch			Today's Trades			
Name	Symbol	Pivot Price	Name	Symbol	Quantity	Price

"'Churning' occurs when a great deal of volume occurs but the price barely advances."

Dow Jones Industrial Average Daily Chart   **1990**

Churning day

Heavy volume

**U.S. equity markets closed
in observance of Thanksgiving Day.**

FRIDAY
26
NOVEMBER
2004

"Handles in cup-with-handle bases that wedge up (drift upwards or more sideways rather than drift downwards) have a much higher probability of failing when they break out to new highs."

Paychex Inc Weekly Chart　　　　　　　　　　　　　　　　**1999**

Handle drifts upward along its lows not downward = "wedging"

Stocks to Watch			Today's Trades			
Name	Symbol	Pivot Price	Name	Symbol	Quantity	Price

SAT/SUN
27/28
NOVEMBER
2004

"On this day in 1998, VeriSign, creators of technology that enabled secure transactions over the Internet, secured a 2,542%, 65-week run after it broke out of a 19-week cup-with-handle formation."

VeriSign Inc Weekly Chart　　　　　　　　　　　　　　　　**1998**

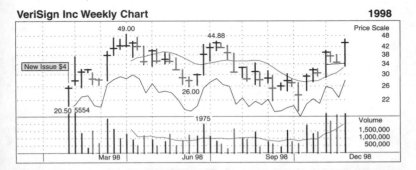

Stocks to Watch			Stocks to Watch		
Name	Symbol	Pivot Price	Name	Symbol	Pivot Price

NOTES:

NOTES:

MONDAY

29

NOVEMBER

2004

"Stocks that have strong runs and then base usually need five weeks of pulling back in order to digest their gains, set up in a base, and go again."

Stocks to Watch			Today's Trades			
Name	Symbol	Pivot Price	Name	Symbol	Quantity	Price

TUESDAY

30

NOVEMBER

2004

"In most but not all cases it's usually a good sign when a company, and especially a small to medium-sized growth company that meets the CAN SLIM criteria, buys its own stock in the open marketplace over a consistent period of time. (A 10% buyback would be considered significant.)"

Stocks to Watch			Today's Trades			
Name	Symbol	Pivot Price	Name	Symbol	Quantity	Price

WEDNESDAY

1

DECEMBER
2004

"Big fund managers generally think the same, and chart patterns generally show their psychology at work."

Stocks to Watch			Today's Trades			
Name	Symbol	Pivot Price	Name	Symbol	Quantity	Price
___	___	___	___	___	___	___
___	___	___	___	___	___	___
___	___	___	___	___	___	___

THURSDAY

2

DECEMBER
2004

"It's normal for growth stocks to create cup patterns during intermediate general market declines and correct 1½ to 2½ times the market averages. Your best choices generally are stocks with base patterns that deteriorate the least during an intermediate market decline."

Stocks to Watch			Today's Trades			
Name	Symbol	Pivot Price	Name	Symbol	Quantity	Price
___	___	___	___	___	___	___
___	___	___	___	___	___	___
___	___	___	___	___	___	___

FRIDAY

3

DECEMBER
2004

"The sight of sluggish or low-priced, lower quality laggards strengthening is a signal to the wise market operator that the upward market move may be near its end. Even turkeys can try to fly in a windstorm."

Stocks to Watch		
Name	Symbol	Pivot Price

Today's Trades			
Name	Symbol	Quantity	Price

SAT/SUN

4/5

DECEMBER
2004

"If, after a successful run, one or two important stocks in a group breaks seriously, the weakness may sooner or later 'wash over' into the remaining stocks in that field."

Stocks to Watch		
Name	Symbol	Pivot Price

Stocks to Watch		
Name	Symbol	Pivot Price

"Handles in a cup-with-handle pattern must form in the upper half of the overall base structure, as measured from the absolute peak of the entire base to the absolute low of the cup. The handle should also be above the stock's 200-day moving average line."

Stocks to Watch			Today's Trades			
Name	Symbol	Pivot Price	Name	Symbol	Quantity	Price

"The market is all about psychology. Chart patterns are essentially maps of psychology, and these chart patterns will remain useful as long as human psychology remains as it is."

Stocks to Watch			Today's Trades			
Name	Symbol	Pivot Price	Name	Symbol	Quantity	Price

WEDNESDAY

8

DECEMBER
2004

"The number one leader is not the largest company or the one with the most recognized brand name; it's the one with the best quarterly and annual earnings growth, return on equity, profit margins, sales growth, price action, and a superior product or service that is gaining market share from older, less innovative competitors."

Stocks to Watch			Today's Trades			
Name	Symbol	Pivot Price	Name	Symbol	Quantity	Price

THURSDAY

9

DECEMBER
2004

"You learn more from your enemies than your friends. Likewise, you learn more from your mistakes than your successes."

Stocks to Watch			Today's Trades			
Name	Symbol	Pivot Price	Name	Symbol	Quantity	Price

FRIDAY
10
DECEMBER
2004

"Never operate from a position of fear. If your stocks are keeping you up at night, sell to the sleeping point!"

Stocks to Watch			Today's Trades			
Name	Symbol	Pivot Price	Name	Symbol	Quantity	Price
___	___	___	___	___	___	___
___	___	___	___	___	___	___
___	___	___	___	___	___	___

SAT/SUN
11/12
DECEMBER
2004

"Don't chase extended stocks. Chasing stocks, like crime, doesn't pay."

Stocks to Watch			Stocks to Watch		
Name	Symbol	Pivot Price	Name	Symbol	Pivot Price
___	___	___	___	___	___
___	___	___	___	___	___
___	___	___	___	___	___

MONDAY
13
DECEMBER
2004

"People tend to buy stocks they like, stocks they feel good about, or stocks they feel comfortable with, but in an otherwise exciting stock market, these sentimental securities often lag the market rather than lead it. Don't just dabble in stocks. Dig in, do some detective work and find out what really works."

Stocks to Watch			Today's Trades			
Name	Symbol	Pivot Price	Name	Symbol	Quantity	Price

TUESDAY
14
DECEMBER
2004

"Jesse Livermore once said, 'There is no bull side or bear side—only the right side.' Which side are you on?"

Stocks to Watch			Today's Trades			
Name	Symbol	Pivot Price	Name	Symbol	Quantity	Price

"Any size capitalization stock can be bought under the CAN SLIM method, but small-cap stocks will be substantially more volatile, both on the upside and downside. From time to time the market will shift its emphasis from small to large caps and vice versa."

Stocks to Watch			Today's Trades			
Name	Symbol	Pivot Price	Name	Symbol	Quantity	Price

"The formation of the handle area in a cup-with-handle base generally takes more than one or two weeks and has a downward price drift or shakeout. Volume will dry up noticeably near the lows in the handle's price pullback phase."

Reebok Intl Ltd Weekly Chart   **1986**

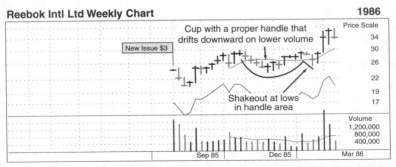

Cup with a proper handle that drifts downward on lower volume

New Issue $3

Shakeout at lows in handle area

Price Scale
34
30
26
22
19
17

Volume
1,200,000
800,000
400,000

Sep 85   Dec 85   Mar 86

Stocks to Watch			Today's Trades			
Name	Symbol	Pivot Price	Name	Symbol	Quantity	Price

"If you notice a company that's doing particularly well, research it thoroughly. In the process, you may discover a supplier company also worth investing in."

Stocks to Watch		
Name	Symbol	Pivot Price

Today's Trades			
Name	Symbol	Quantity	Price

"On December 18, 1998, Emulex Corp., maker of fiber-channel products that increased the flow of information across computer networks busted out of a high, tight, four-week flag formation and zoomed 3,023% over the next 66 weeks."

Emulex Corp Weekly Chart   **1998**

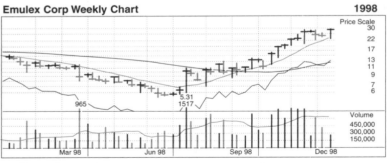

Stocks to Watch		
Name	Symbol	Pivot Price

Stocks to Watch		
Name	Symbol	Pivot Price

"Of the most successful stocks from 1953 through 1993, nearly two out of three were part of group advances. So remember, the importance of staying on top of your research and being aware of new group movements cannot be overestimated."

Stocks to Watch			Today's Trades			
Name	Symbol	Pivot Price	Name	Symbol	Quantity	Price

"Boom times in the fiberoptic industry drove JDS Uniphase out of a 21-week cup-with-handle chart base on this date in 1998, resulting in a booming 2,132% run for the stock in only 20 weeks."

JDS Uniphase Corp Weekly Chart   **1998**

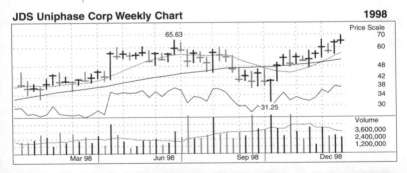

Stocks to Watch			Today's Trades			
Name	Symbol	Pivot Price	Name	Symbol	Quantity	Price

"Sometimes after a stock breaks out, it is unable to advance due to a declining general market and builds a second base in the area just on top of the previous base. When the market turns bullish, this stock is apt to be one of the first to emerge at a new high en route to a huge gain."

Oracle Corp Weekly Chart   **1999**

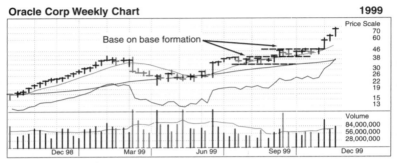

Base on base formation

"Corrections in the market are a 'feedback phase.' Use the action in the indexes and leading stocks as market feedback, e.g., what is weak, what is strong, what is basing and what is breaking down."

Stocks to Watch		
Name	Symbol	Pivot Price

Today's Trades			
Name	Symbol	Quantity	Price

Stocks to Watch		
Name	Symbol	Pivot Price

Today's Trades			
Name	Symbol	Quantity	Price

"Avoid buying any stock unless its strength and attractiveness are confirmed by at least one other important stock in the same group. You can get away without such confirmation in a few cases where the company does something truly unique unto itself, but these are very few in number."

U.S. equity markets closed in observance of Christmas.

"Cups without handles have a somewhat higher failure rate."

Ryland Group Inc Weekly Chart   **2002**

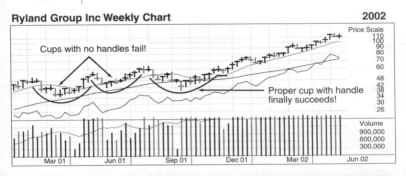

Stocks to Watch		
Name	Symbol	Pivot Price

Stocks to Watch		
Name	Symbol	Pivot Price

"Analyze the quality of sponsorship. Know who the sponsors are and more importantly, look for stock held by at least one or two of the more savvy portfolio managers who have the best performance records."

Stocks to Watch			Today's Trades			
Name	Symbol	Pivot Price	Name	Symbol	Quantity	Price

"After the first break down, some stocks may pull back up in price one time. This provides an opportunity to sell shares."

Stocks to Watch			Today's Trades			
Name	Symbol	Pivot Price	Name	Symbol	Quantity	Price

WEDNESDAY
29
DECEMBER
2004

"On this date in 1997, Internet company incubator CMGI emerged from a 13-week cup-with-handle base to rocket an astounding 8,729% over the next two years."

CMGI Inc Weekly Chart   **1997**

Stocks to Watch			Today's Trades			
<u>Name</u>	<u>Symbol</u>	<u>Pivot Price</u>	<u>Name</u>	<u>Symbol</u>	<u>Quantity</u>	<u>Price</u>

THURSDAY
30
DECEMBER
2004

"During bear markets certain leading stocks will seem to be bucking the trend by holding up in price and creating the impression of strength, but what you're seeing is just a postponement of the inevitable. Eventually all the leaders will succumb to the selling."

Stocks to Watch			Today's Trades			
<u>Name</u>	<u>Symbol</u>	<u>Pivot Price</u>	<u>Name</u>	<u>Symbol</u>	<u>Quantity</u>	<u>Price</u>

"Stocks coming straight off the bottom of a cup pattern into new highs without first forming a handle are frequently more risky."

Ciber Inc Weekly Chart 1997

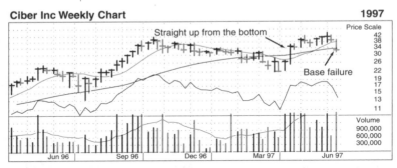

Stocks to Watch			Today's Trades			
Name	Symbol	Pivot Price	Name	Symbol	Quantity	Price

"From time to time, when trying to evaluate the general market or individual stocks, ask yourself, 'What does *everyone* know?' If everyone 'knows' that a stock is 'overvalued' and is about to go down in flames, or if everyone 'knows' that the U.S. economy is heading into a deflationary spiral and seven years of depression, it probably isn't."

Stocks to Watch			Stocks to Watch		
Name	Symbol	Pivot Price	Name	Symbol	Pivot Price

2003

January

S	M	T	W	T	F	S
			1	2	3	4
5	6	7	8	9	10	11
12	13	14	15	16	17	18
19	20	21	22	23	24	25
26	27	28	29	30	31	

February

S	M	T	W	T	F	S
						1
2	3	4	5	6	7	8
9	10	11	12	13	14	15
16	17	18	19	20	21	22
23	24	25	26	27	28	

March

S	M	T	W	T	F	S
						1
2	3	4	5	6	7	8
9	10	11	12	13	14	15
16	17	18	19	20	21	22
$^{23}/_{30}$	$^{24}/_{31}$	25	26	27	28	29

April

S	M	T	W	T	F	S
		1	2	3	4	5
6	7	8	9	10	11	12
13	14	15	16	17	18	19
20	21	22	23	24	25	26
27	28	29	30			

May

S	M	T	W	T	F	S
				1	2	3
4	5	6	7	8	9	10
11	12	13	14	15	16	17
18	19	20	21	22	23	24
25	26	27	28	29	30	31

June

S	M	T	W	T	F	S
1	2	3	4	5	6	7
8	9	10	11	12	13	14
15	16	17	18	19	20	21
22	23	24	25	26	27	28
29	30					

July

S	M	T	W	T	F	S
		1	2	3	4	5
6	7	8	9	10	11	12
13	14	15	16	17	18	19
20	21	22	23	24	25	26
27	28	29	30	31		

August

S	M	T	W	T	F	S
					1	2
3	4	5	6	7	8	9
10	11	12	13	14	15	16
17	18	19	20	21	22	23
$^{24}/_{31}$	25	26	27	28	29	30

September

S	M	T	W	T	F	S
	1	2	3	4	5	6
7	8	9	10	11	12	13
14	15	16	17	18	19	20
21	22	23	24	25	26	27
28	29	30				

October

S	M	T	W	T	F	S
			1	2	3	4
5	6	7	8	9	10	11
12	13	14	15	16	17	18
19	20	21	22	23	24	25
26	27	28	29	30	31	

November

S	M	T	W	T	F	S
						1
2	3	4	5	6	7	8
9	10	11	12	13	14	15
16	17	18	19	20	21	22
$^{23}/_{30}$	24	25	26	27	28	29

December

S	M	T	W	T	F	S
	1	2	3	4	5	6
7	8	9	10	11	12	13
14	15	16	17	18	19	20
21	22	23	24	25	26	27
28	29	30	31			

2004

January
S	M	T	W	T	F	S
				1	2	3
4	5	6	7	8	9	10
11	12	13	14	15	16	17
18	19	20	21	22	23	24
25	26	27	28	29	30	31

February
S	M	T	W	T	F	S
1	2	3	4	5	6	7
8	9	10	11	12	13	14
15	16	17	18	19	20	21
22	23	24	25	26	27	28

March
S	M	T	W	T	F	S
	1	2	3	4	5	6
7	8	9	10	11	12	13
14	15	16	17	18	19	20
21	22	23	24	25	26	27
28	29	30	31			

April
S	M	T	W	T	F	S
				1	2	3
4	5	6	7	8	9	10
11	12	13	14	15	16	17
18	19	20	21	22	23	24
25	26	27	28	29	30	

May
S	M	T	W	T	F	S
						1
2	3	4	5	6	7	8
9	10	11	12	13	14	15
16	17	18	19	20	21	22
$23/_{30}$	$24/_{31}$	25	26	27	28	29

June
S	M	T	W	T	F	S
		1	2	3	4	5
6	7	8	9	10	11	12
13	14	15	16	17	18	19
20	21	22	23	24	25	26
27	28	29	30			

July
S	M	T	W	T	F	S
				1	2	3
4	5	6	7	8	9	10
11	12	13	14	15	16	17
18	19	20	21	22	23	24
25	26	27	28	29	30	31

August
S	M	T	W	T	F	S
1	2	3	4	5	6	7
89	10	11	12	13	14	15
16	17	18	19	20	21	22
23	24	25	26	27	28	29
30	31					

September
S	M	T	W	T	F	S
			1	2	3	4
5	6	7	8	9	10	11
12	13	14	15	16	17	18
19	20	21	22	23	24	25
26	27	28	29	30		

October
S	M	T	W	T	F	S
					1	2
3	4	5	6	7	8	9
10	11	12	13	14	15	16
17	18	19	20	21	22	23
$24/_{31}$	25	26	27	28	29	30

November
S	M	T	W	T	F	S
	1	2	3	4	5	6
7	8	9	10	11	12	13
14	15	16	17	18	19	20
21	22	23	24	25	26	27
28	29	30				

December
S	M	T	W	T	F	S
		1	2	3	4
5	6	7	8	9	10	11
12	13	14	15	16	17	18
19	20	21	22	23	24	25
26	27	28	29	30	31	

2005

January
S	M	T	W	T	F	S
						1
2	3	4	5	6	7	8
9	10	11	12	13	14	15
16	17	18	19	20	21	22
$^{23}/_{30}$	$^{24}/_{31}$	25	26	27	28	29

February
S	M	T	W	T	F	S
		1	2	3	4	5
6	7	8	9	10	11	12
13	14	15	16	17	18	19
20	21	22	23	24	25	26
27	28					

March
S	M	T	W	T	F	S
		1	2	3	4	5
6	7	8	9	10	11	12
13	14	15	16	17	18	19
20	21	22	23	24	25	26
27	28	29	30	31		

April
S	M	T	W	T	F	S
					1	2
3	4	5	6	7	8	9
10	11	12	13	14	15	16
17	18	19	20	21	22	23
24	25	26	27	28	29	30

May
S	M	T	W	T	F	S
1	2	3	4	5	6	7
8	9	10	11	12	13	14
15	16	17	18	19	20	21
22	23	24	25	26	27	28
29	30	31				

June
S	M	T	W	T	F	S
			1	2	3	4
5	6	7	8	9	10	11
12	13	14	15	16	17	18
19	20	21	22	23	24	25
26	27	28	29	30		

July
S	M	T	W	T	F	S
					1	2
3	4	5	6	7	8	9
10	11	12	13	14	15	16
17	18	19	20	21	22	23
$^{24}/_{31}$	25	26	27	28	29	30

August
S	M	T	W	T	F	S
	1	2	3	4	5	6
7	8	9	10	11	12	13
14	15	16	17	18	19	20
21	22	23	24	25	26	27
28	29	30	31			

September
S	M	T	W	T	F	S
				1	2	3
4	5	6	7	8	9	10
11	12	13	14	15	16	17
18	19	20	21	22	23	24
25	26	27	28	29	30	

October
S	M	T	W	T	F	S
						1
2	3	4	5	6	7	8
9	10	11	12	13	14	15
16	17	18	19	20	21	22
$^{23}/_{30}$	$^{24}/_{31}$	25	26	27	28	29

November
S	M	T	W	T	F	S
		1	2	3	4	5
6	7	8	9	10	11	12
13	14	15	16	17	18	19
20	21	22	23	24	25	26
27	28	29	30			

December
S	M	T	W	T	F	S
				1	2	3
4	5	6	7	8	9	10
11	12	13	14	15	16	17
18	19	20	21	22	23	24
25	26	27	28	29	30	31

NOTES:

NOTES:

NOTES: